Brya Faith Lee has a Bachelor of Fine Arts Degree from the University of Massachusetts and attended Smith College for Chinese Art History and Design through the Five-College Exchange Student Consortium. For over a decade, Brya worked with special need individuals in academic settings and as a horticulture therapist at Smith College Lyman Plant House Conservatory through a local inclusion agency. Brya has been at Inspirit Crystals in Northampton, MA., for the past six years as a Tarot Reader, and previously eight years at a renowned resort in the Berkshires with guests from around the world as a lecturer in the Metaphysical Department. Brya received her Massage and Thai Yoga certifications from Kripalu Center for Yoga and Health in Lenox, MA., in 2002. Brya brings her 19th-century Tibetan Singing Bowls to the Christopher Heights Community for sound therapy, in her town of Northampton. In 1993, Brya was certified with Hospice of Hampshire County. Brya loves doing artwork, botany, birds, the ocean and walking barefoot at the Quabbin.

Memorial of Mayril Lee Fowler, a bird lover, tree-hugging-hippy with Martin Luther King posters for her adopted son in his room, for her devotion to eight children, sewing expertise, design exemplar, heart of gold and singing voice as sweet as heaven. She wanted a world without weapons. Calm.

Brya Faith Lee

THE DYING ART

AUSTIN MACAULEY PUBLISHERS®

LONDON • CAMBRIDGE • NEW YORK • SHARJAH

Ordering Information
Quantity sales: Special discounts are available on quantity purchases by corporations, associations, and others. For details, contact the publisher at the address below.

Publisher's Cataloging-in-Publication data
Lee, Brya Faith
The Dying Art

ISBN 9798886935578 (Paperback)
ISBN 9798886935592 (ePub e-book)
ISBN 9798886935585 (Audiobook)

Library of Congress Control Number: 2024909508

www.austinmacauleyusa.com

First Published 2024
Austin Macauley Publishers LLC
40 Wall Street, 33rd Floor, Suite 3302
New York, NY 10005
USA

mail-usa@austinmacauley.com
+1 (646) 512576

20250818

To Charlie and Cybele Derby for their lifelong friendship, generosity, great YouTube wild edible plant resources and for many captivating, memorable stories and songs around Native American Indians, dreams, and premonitions.

To my sons, Elan Bonde and Austin Miles, for all your national and state awards in sports, award scholarships in philosophy, drumming talents exemplar and as higher contemplations of life, authors. Like twins you both share but could not be more different; one a gentle yet passionate humanitarian and my other son a diligent diplomatic empath.

And also to Christopher Baker, a gracious spiritual master with invaluable expertise in human relations etiquette. To Clara at the River Valley CO-OP for her open ear.
Anne Faith for her expertise in storytelling.

Table of Contents

Prologue
Voices from the Heart

There are no words to express when a loved one passes over. We are silent. They are silent, or so it seems. Our minds take over and grief ensues in a downward spiral. It's a strong message the beating heart incurs, a mixture of regrets and doubts from our dead-end thinking. The heart, however, has been found to have a mini brain, to have sensory cells that think, feel, and remember, called neurites. This is where memories of loved ones remain, recorded independent of the cranial brain. The sound and rhythm of our loved ones' voices last forever in the heart. Because, who really dies?

It is not them; they live on in the light, but it is us. We need to find compassion for ourselves, to feel an inner loving freedom again, through embracing our hearts and giving it a voice, not to make it go away, not to make it silent, but to bring this grief to a loving stillness. We need to learn to take the last threads of love we had with that person, that tiny crumb, final link, still grieving in us, back home, from head to the heart, from bound love to boundless again.

"It is essential to be hidden
But a miracle to be found"
D.W. Winnicott

Out of the Box

I first appear out of a box via U.S. Mail, on an envelope addressed to my father, Bryce F. Lee. My mother, Mayril, is seven months pregnant and searching for names. Mayril notices the c and e running together into a cursive a, forming Brya, from his name Bryce. Mayril is derived from her parents' blending of Thelma with Cyril. Even though Mayril invented my name, I wanted to see if it was anywhere else in the world. I found out Brya is a genus of a species of flowering tree in the pea family, Fabaceae. Horticulturally, it is a tropical plant in the Caribbean Islands, known as the Jamaican Rain Tree. Natives see Brya as a harbinger of rain, blossoming just moments before in golden clusters, along arching branches.

Faith, my middle name, means one is devoted to the invisible, to trusting in deeply spiritual values and developing a centering love and light as the highest possible human virtues, becoming an inner flame, of which evidence of proof, has yet to be found; Hebrews 11:1. Our life is as much a question as an answer. Birth and death seem to be taking us through the same place, unfolding like a lotus, in a myriad of forms, while remaining whole, in a structure, a template, from the full spectrum of colors and sound, an orchestration, a palette, a painting, a forever blossoming canvas we are living in.

Life is a constant dying to the self, to what we think we know, to embracing the universal common thread of love in its wholeness at the heart of all existence. The heart of matter. How matter forms, from sound from the word, from this dendritic pattern seen in the Tree of Life. Death is right here. We think we are going to die later, tomorrow, or next year, but when it happens, it's right now, this is it. Life never dies, but the art of dying shows us, as also birth does; that love is inseparable and both are designed to do the same thing, surrender to the ever-expanding evolution of consciousness, of universal love built into all things. Dying is an innate cycle of life that is ever-expanding awareness, past all our thinking, concepts, and words, to the essential spark of life. To the life force itself which is free from our thoughts. Death is for those that are here, that are left behind. A jumping off place for evolution.

The body is really an empty vessel with God expressing itself, through this creative form, we call life. The life force itself is a forever moving river, a river of love. God is an artist, and the brush strokes are sounds all around us from inside the womb and all throughout life, and through the veil to the other side, we use our heart, voices from the heart to connect. This word, this sound, never dies, for sound can transfer through matter, opening space. Sound is the static form of life, and awareness or Consciousness is a matter of how much room you have in your heart, carved out through thick and thin experiences, through healing a heartbreak. This invisible stillness moving us with great passion, with every beat, keeps this sound, this space this word, this thread of light throughout all existence, as the ocean goes from high tide to low tide, continuum. So strong, so deep is this life force we can see a soft, green plant budding up through cement. The love from a loved one is the same moving love from your own heart, the two are one central flame with or without the physical body, this thread still lives, in deep peace. This thread of light continues to all our ancestors that have ever lived are in the voices from the heart, herein.

Standing Still

I grew up alone, together, in a ranch at 1137 Long Hill Road in Cheshire, Ct. There were nine of us, total. It was a small city, a metropolis, one sibling after the other, like clockwork, like an assembly line. I was sibling number three. Mayril was industrial at love.

"Let's go…get up," Bryce said, waking us at midnight and escorting everyone down the steps in single file. We were clasping hold of the one in front, while the free hands were trying to find the iron railing. Walking across the lawn, we could feel the grass folding beneath our zipper-footed pajamas. Bryce then said, "Now everyone, look up."

In an instant flat, I figured out I have now been everywhere possible, even light years away, even stars long gone, I got to see, I got to go, I got to meet, right here, without even moving, standing still. I did not know if it fit all into me, or all of me into it.

The night sky was a deep, dark, rich, fertile blackness of restful peace, like a womb, like a mother. In the darkness I found my own personal light dwells inside me. Looking up at the stars, I could see they have done it. They live happily in the dark. Alone together, they found their own light, in clusters, like us the Lee family.

The sun blinds our own inner light during the day, but in the night, we find it looking up into the stars, up into the dark, we feel the life force and it ignites us with the higher spirit, the pure wonder, the deepest appreciation of existence becomes a circuitry of love. The connection to all things, all places, all feelings, all life and in any timelines of existence. In the light of day, our sun's rays are blinding and bidding us to do this, to do that, like a moth to a flame, a path already magnetizing us to follow. But in the night, we see that all things are merged, no agendas taking place, just the all-expansive awe of the magnitude of infinite space all around us, embracing our soul, like a giant hug, and our relationship with life switches in the dark, in the night, we now see something far more. Meaning that we feel the shedding of what we think we know, what our thoughts don't say, going back to a surrender to what we know we know without even thinking. Says it all, in the truth in every day.

Tied to the Trees

Mayril tied me to the trees, pulling a suspender vest down over my head then clasping it to a bungie cord attached to one of the three shaggy pines out front. She went back inside into the overspill of youngsters to watch me from the giant bay window.

After stretching as far as I could go, I found myself turned around, dancing face to face with the Standing Ones, the tree Elders. Their soft, smooth layers which overlap like the scales of a fish, with fringed curled edges like wings of a bird. I see maple leaves floating in the air ascend into birds flying, descending leaves into a pond, transforming into fish fins. Life camouflages, life is a vision, a pattern of art. Interwoven. Always dying to be born.

Suddenly, a bird is chirping; as I spot this beauty, it confirms in unison, in synchronicity. The whole connection, that if you are open to it, it becomes more into one's reality, a fact that everything around us is always communicating.

Touching its smooth, plush, curled-up, outer layers of bark, my fingers become stuck together. I did not know which was stronger. Was it the ambient strong scent of the sap with its piercing aroma to my nose, or its powerfully magnetic, transparent, amber colored glue, of a mere drop possessed? Nature is so diverse, we never have to study it, when its every surprise is a wealth of knowledge connecting us, like a glue, into the fabric of life, weaving.

The Egyptians rubbed amber for its static charge. Standing Ones spoke silently, but in this sphere of wonder I could hear their words whispering with the wind.

Here, I met the walking stick, the praying mantis and the daddy long leg. They knew to stay clear of the sap. But not me. The invisible can still be strong even if you cannot see it. Like faith is. Faith is clear, it is invisible, yet one of the strongest threads or light rays within the spiritual glue of life, strong as iron, clear as the eternal sky.

The pointed pine needles fallen on the ground are sticking in clumps to the bottom of my bare feet, while walking I am balancing their communications with my movements, juggling back into the house, in a loud silence, while listening. My heart is on fire with sounds of nature, with its communication, therein, for I had contacted Spirit and we were now singing, silently together from the heart. As the birds do each morning, at dawn, chattering together in unique calls, communicating in their own languages. I wonder what exactly they are saying. Then, I melt into their energy, their excitement for life at first rays of sun as it reaches not just my ears, by my heart, opens in the asking, and joy enters instead. Joy from their expression emitting into the first rays of sun, into the first touchdowns of photosynthesis, and it dawns on me, they are clearing all the debris in my head to my own repetitive thinking. It's a song, it's healing. It's a morning, mourning, bidding yesterday gone.

To see all life as an art form with the beauty of diversity all saying the same thing, life is a moving stillness, both in one. When we think of stillness, we think of silence but instead, stillness is love in action.

Tub time I went in splashing water over the side as my mother whisked out the older two sisters like they were dolls, one under each arm, sideways out the door. Then her cracked blood-stained knuckles from so many dishes and cleaning came back in front of my face and pulled the plug.

Tub time became a tundra with very loud roaring lions coming from the suction of water mixing with air and funnels forming in the wake of its inertia down the drain and mirroring echoes off the tiled walls and floor, as the tornado was taking in its last gasping gulps to die just as soon as being born. I could not change its fate, even with my still stuck together fingers like a mitten now playing with the funnel, its destiny remained, as it morphed over to one side it was still being sucked down through the pipes and silenced somewhere under the house then out front to water the pines. I yawned, a tiger's yawn, then went running through the house, drying off. Shush, shushshshshsh were the repeated words from our mother for the overspill of children, you could be sure, a youngster was sleeping in our inner city in the small ranch at the top of the hill in the metropolis, where I lived.

Tiptoeing around like a ballerina, I did jump up and down to hear the swishing of the water in my stomach. Sounding just like when you shake a coconut. It was a quiet thing I thought only I could hear, until everyone breaks out into laughter, and we hear the proverbial hush warnings, shush, shush, shush, again and again. The mantra of seven times for seven siblings from our beloved mother, Mayril. Bedtime was upon us. Rounding up the herd was the next mantra of 'Hurry Up, Hurry Up'. This is all we knew on the inside, in the sanctuary of home, in the cave, in the wallpapered arcade of playing graduated downward the three girls, then the three boys, then a girl at the tail end, who came in like a comet.

These two mantras throughout the day, intermixed, without any real purpose, rhyme, or reason, our mother would suddenly insist. This was her sign she existed somewhere in the cluster of us young stars, I mean youngsters, she was somehow a human, a person, with something to say, projecting into our little lives her own frayed nerves, but we survived. She would always say, she believed, "sticks and stones will break our bones, but names will always hurt us." That we heal much faster from physical wounds than the emotional ones, which tend to linger on and on. The unseen seems to stay longer and require healing powers that are not biologically inbuilt as scabs are, involuntary innate.

Healing the soul, with self-love, acceptance, allowance, takes, making, an inner space to feel it all, the bad and the good, with an eye of equal unconditional awareness, an embracing, like the womb, where it is safe, a dark room, filled with all love, the unity of life, the unity of all thought, is the heart, merges with compassion. That is why our mother, when we and other children in our neighborhood swore once, and they were paddled and grounded. Our mother just said to us, "don't do it again." Within minutes, the phone rang off the wall from the neighborhood parents, all calling Mayril to say she should punish us. Mayril replied clearly to them that she was against that method and she made sure to say to them that punishment would make it stand out, make it remembered, and then the child may end up swearing more; that abuse leads to more abuse and refused their behavior modification methods. From us, on the inside, we really all loved her way of thinking and made us want to be better people, to be just like her. Later studies showed that the abusive partner in a relationship mostly came from a family of physical punishment, and it became banned and illegal. Our mother was a progressive, protective soul for all people, every race and creed, for human equality, prophetic.

At dusk, Bryce Sr., would cup his hands, creating a hollowed centered space then would blow into his soft large palms, calling us, and out came the sound just like an owl—whoo, whooo, whoooo. When we heard that, we'd run from all quadrants of the neighborhood to the backyard. We then had a head count while we were trying to do the owl call, copying our dad, without fail, we couldn't emulate it yet; we then caught a few fireflies with him, and then we let them go flickering their pulsating light; signals for propagation, and ran inside to the picnic table for another night of spaghetti, with our mantra mother, Mayril.

That explains my innate fascination with the owl, its echoing invisible hoots in the dark, inviting, seductive sounds one can be both asleep and hear simultaneously, like one is awake, from both states of mind. Its sound weaves an alluring call permeating the forest through your opened window, late at night. The odd sound they make, in a certain off-key measure, could be to find food with unsuspecting creatures that follow that tune, perhaps hypnotized into being curious.

Just like dolphins create while jumping out making arches from the water to the air, creating a palpable electricity of joy, the movement ignites negative and positive ions, spreading throughout their field of water.

As the eagle and hawk on the ethers do, floating, without flapping a wing, the 8, a symbol of eternity, back and forth, perhaps opening the portals to heaven. I wondered, one time, why the Robins were jumping around on the grass, on a very dry day. Then, I realized they are imitating the behavior of rain, each hop is like the tapping of drops coming down, alluring the worms to come up for a drink.

My father awakened me to the space of stars, the all-pervasive darkness holding up the light without tire, endlessly, forever, living in the grace of this Being of LOVE, the unity of space and light, together, in the air of the night sky with her warm gentle all absorbing presence, was its giant all-encompassing hug, of pure black, powerful, fertile, potential all around us, demonstrating how all imagination is possible, nothing is impossible for even in the word impossible writes; I'm possible.

Just like in photography, when one goes into a darkroom. Expectant of the film to develop each object separately, you slide the paper into the silver solution, into the liquid, into the water and it develops all at once. This is life. Life is a pre-ordained grid. Life is all electrical. Even the ant is connected to human evolution directly, its development transposes with us in symbiosis and homeostasis, the RNA and the DNA the immediate environmental weaved with the ancient lineage, residing in this same pattern of neural pathways we see in the universe and we see in the brain, cat scans are the same as the mycelium fugus beneath us, as too are the patterns of trees and even our fingerprints, the placenta, and of lightning. The spark of life in matter. The Spirit, from the soil, a soul ignites, from the deep dark earth the body is formed.

No past we can put our hand on, in no future do we ever come to, only here we are, standing still, spinning, running to the same place, when we get there, it's the same space we left from. Tomorrow never comes. The past and future are the same exact place, here.

This mystery has one constant fact, this is the fuel that forms energy into structure. Perhaps finding the fact of why this mystery is, would stop life, end existence. That's what are minds, our thoughts try to do, and it gets in the way of the truth, the truth that: in truth we do not know what anything really is, not a doctor, not a lawyer, not a president, nor a priest or scientist, knows what a single thing is, or what made it or where and why it came to be. Life is a great mystery, an awe of beauty, diversity and as it is unfolding, this work of art, of creation, we move with it and other times, we grow with it and other times we die to it, is all the same space.

We cannot put our hands nor one thought on a sum degree, because ultimately, we are that answer. That question has the answer all in one heartbeat. There is sound and color and it is negative and positive electrons, our body and mind, thoughts and feelings, heart and soul can ignite within, into one, into love. The negative has bad connotations and associations, but should be about rest, going deeper into making space and subsequent peace, inside us, from the heart, like the womb where there is all sound, a surround sound starting at the first fetal formation of a heartbeat.

The light is positive and active. We have combined our language into prejudice, and it is not just evident in racism but our actual words and phrases like, blackmail; why don't we say whitemail? Because black is not understood, its purpose, its meaning, its spiritual significance is important in learning, in realizing black is the combination of all color and white is the absence. A force of unity, a powerful peace, rest. Which reverses with less density and black is then, absence and white is the combination of a full spectrum. As also in the role of relationships, which tries to clear ways to open, to unravel the conflict between emotions and thinking and the sexes continuing evolution to wholeness, a challenge of surrender, of dying to what we think and becoming what we feel, our steps of evolution.

We can use communication and compassionate listening in communing deeper with loved ones and with those passed over, a more lasting connection, based on the sound of expressing our feelings, into and through emotional intelligence. Love does what is best for our loved ones and they would want to do best by us, they open grief in us as a weight, an anchor of importance, to the gravity of love, which is to expand our capacity past egoic love, the mind, and thinking, to its pure awareness, a 'la sustantifique moelle'.

Personal love is still linked to universal love. The pain we feel with a broken heart is from love. Love is at the core of that pain. It resides under, in the middle, behind that pain. When we have cuts or broken bones, the scars from this are our own injuries or falling down, but all heartache is love in reverse, it's a crack in our amour.

Death has had fear attached to it all of our lives. With warning words of 'watch out' while crossing the road, you might get hit and die, or don't play with fire, or that disease will end your life. This association to death is deeply engrained. Thus, it is hard to separate the feeling of grief in our heart, that it is the mind's filter and that feeling we have is actually the exact amount of love one had for them, stored in the heart.

There is no cut, no scar, no bleeding. There is nothing bad happening there. The stress in the mind, a loss for words, is pointing to the heart. The crack in the heart is where love can get back in. We can seal our hearts with our own love, then reach the higher love our loved ones in heaven are feeling right now. Open to this two-way street, exchange of energy always, is available. Again, another exchange but without their human body, it is much easier to connect by placing both hands on the heart when feeling grief, and be open, just listen, just allow, just be present, be glad you are alive to experience such love, the essence of life, this love, through the deceased, this is trying to reach you, to turn this pain around as a sanctimony. Witness grief subside through self-love, through our own compassion, through clearing our own energy, right now right here.

Otherwise, we can't embrace the truth. The mind becomes a trap, chained down with dead-end words. Instead, it is in the heartbeat that transforms us, love evolves. Keeping it open using compassion or self-love on oneself allows the feeling to just rest, to just be, to survive in the cave of the heart, the sanctuary of all life. Their love can return. The light of love, it has wings, in the timeless beating of the heart, a point of connection, remains. Behind every pain in the heart, is the original source of love, the common thread to all existence. We can close this grief, not by stopping our thinking but by surpassing all limitations of the mind, its beliefs, and misconceptions around what we call pain. Love is nameless.

It's a matter of mechanics and chemistry, so life force can flow through denser forms and still have freedom.

We can learn to love our pain. Not to be afraid of emotions, because their purpose is to hollow us out. To deepen our capacity for more light to go within us.

Life does not come at birth, it already is; death doesn't stop anything, the two are always at the same point. The point of truth; that we are embodiments of a living light, an invisible powerful love, a moving grace.

The objective mind only goes so far, but the subjective heart is the true meaning of what keeps life moving, the real significance. Truly, something to honor, the emotions of life is the life force itself.

Words of Wisdom

However, the first words of wisdom came from the mouth of my mother, Mayril. She said all things turn back around, all thought, judgment, deed, action, come back to us. Like a boomerang. Mayril said that it may not be now, it could come back later in another lifetime, and that we are souls in a body, and in each life, we drop it like a costume. This is when I first heard this word. This word was Karma, at age seven.

That must be why, looking back, I married Stephen in the second grade, twice. The first time was to show him respect for his bold, bright spirit shining from his sparkling eyes, 'oel ngati kameie,' and his wide ear-to-ear smile. Because, if what my mother proclaimed was true, that our bodies don't matter, that our bodies are just a costume and the soul is what counts, the inside, and if what she said about Karma, was even remotely real, then the soul should be honored. I then, without pointing out certain classmates, or they might come back in their next lifetime with a wide space between their two front teeth, and I, just in case, no one knew about this underlying truth, had to marry him; it was a serious fated precautionary measure, I just had to take, given this information I was learning via Mantra Mother Mayril.

Mantra Mother Mayril

My mother also said, time and time again, to put yourself into other people's shoes. Try to understand how they feel. Acknowledge that we are a soul, the light of the world is within, the same and equal in each person, tree, animal, bird, insect, rock. That was my upbringing, and everything on earth has a soul and is all alive as one living being. The I in me is the same I in you. The fertile soil, the soul. Electrical light of love, as in all life, is this DNA thread, interweaving a canvas, a landscape, a creative art of dance.

"Brya, there isn't any intelligence in matter; all is all and all. An all-inclusive fabric throughout existence," said Mayril from the Key to the Scriptures by Mary Baker Eddy.

It's a design, a perfect propagating structure, with freedom inside to feel whatever, dream whatever, our own will, to feel the light within. To mold a soul. To grow a spirit. To keep going through from within.

Every year at Halloween, Mayril designed, sewed, and won first, second, and third place, awarded with silver and gold coin dollars. We were straight out of a Hollywood movie scene. I was Little Bo Peep with curly locks, seersucker apron, button-down full skirt and a lamb in tow on wheels. The following year, I was a monkey with a long, three-foot tail of flattened cardboard inside, curling up at the end and waving behind me.

Like Mayril said, we are souls and we drop our outer shell, our skin, our body when we ascend to another life, here on earth, here under the sky of heaven. As she told me these messages, I would be using a protractor then getting it caught sticking out through my palm from the sharp pointed needle between my fingers to the other side of my hand. While she made her point, I was experiencing acupuncture. "There really is no set point to life, but that does not mean it is pointless," she said. Gratitude and practicing thankfulness are not words, but waves, feelings that come back to us, we create our own energy.

I remember a session in Raja Yoga. After chanting the violet flame intonations, waking up in my dreaming that night, seeing myself in a pool or ocean of tranquility, floating like a cocoon with only the shapes of human bodies, like a mummy wrapped in silk, many bodies floating, in many rows, and this emanating peaceful loving vibration was surrounding and feeding us, we were refueling directly on god's love in the deep dark fertile black potential of a powerfully peaceful sky.

Early on, my mother got me the 8 ball. It was black with the number 8 in a white circle. You shake while asking a question. An answer would float up in a viscous cloud, surfacing into its triangular window.

I was also given Chinese Fortune Sticks. They came in a tin canister with an oracle book. You start by asking a question. It says to shake it with a flick of the wrist, tipping it over, side to side, then try to drop only one out. If two or more fall out, attempt it again, repeat.

Or an alternative was to while asking a question and shaking the canister, hearing the thug, thug, thug, I was instructed to pour them all out. The sticks piled up into a mingled, interwoven nest in front of me on the floor. I had to carefully, thoughtfully, breathing calmly in a coordinated effort find the one most eligible to free it from entanglement without disturbing the bunch. It was like living in the metropolis; don't disturb each other, now it's with a bunch of bamboo sticks and their numbers.

The 64 thin bamboo sticks with pale, thin, red digits on each end would pile up into a nested jumbled heap, it was Zen, the one that stood out, the one that I could take, that one, that very one, was the only real answer to my question, and it worked.

This was my beginnings. A fine-tuning into the unknown. A delicate operation between body and mind, practicing intuition, developing subsequent cultivation of an inner trust with the whole world around me, in the city where I lived, all-inclusive home.

Otherwise, Mayril, besides the assembly line of kids, was making sequenced shirts for me, of birds, and a wool, maxi length cape lined with silk. It had one large button at the top with a looped, twine hook.

My long hair got stuck in the hood. So heavy was this deep maroon cape, it weighed more than me, cloaking me, but forcing me to feel more visible in myself, somewhere inside.

When the tiny naked trolls came out, with hair standing on end, Mayril made them miniature felt outfits and sold them by the dozens to Malley's and Macy's in New Haven, CT. Up until a factory got wind of her idea and took over making the trolls' attire and she was ousted. Like an assembly line with her fingers covered in eczema, sore and chafed. She also made lace-covered bottles using sap for the glue and an unfolded burlap flower. Taking one thread and pulling it out, petals formed. It was "flower power" back then. "I am loved."

Our woody station wagon was on its last legs, so our father said we could paint giant flowers on it. It was the only one in the universe that had flower power and I am Loved in giant letters, as we drove around.

Otherwise, all of us were escorted to Camp Berger in Winchester, CT., each year. It gave our parents a break. The Grange Hall we attended for square dancing sponsored us, which also had dance on Saturday nights with songs like: Cherish is the One, See you in September.

It was Indian pow-wow night on Fridays where we all painted our faces and went to the lake to put candles on the water, sending them floating out. So rich was the camp next door, behind the tall fence, with their motorboats and we had just row boats, you could hear their loud, intrusive, intercom system telling everyone there what to do. I liked being on the poor side. It was much better over here, this side of the tall wooden fence that I tried to look through to see what all the noise was about. The noise was their daily life, their camp experienced as seen from the rich, so sad, so intrusive, feeling how my camp was real. They raced around on the lake, speeding, causing giant waves.

I liked our canoes better because they were quiet. Their boats were causing a wake during our swimming lessons, and instead of doing the crawl or breathe stroke we were coming up for air, choking on waves smashing into our faces. Each of us had a credit of seven dollars for snacks per week. By the time Bryce came to visit, we would be in the minus twenty-one dollars, times seven, times four weeks. It was for orange popsicles and Hershey's M&Ms, mosquito repellent, poison ivy lotion, and soda pop drinks.

I favored the crafts classes with copper foil rubbing, tile hot plate, and macramé making. We also used the wood burner to carve faces into what was called a tiki then thread a suede string and hang it around our neck like a mini totem pole. Archery came easy. I liked how it taught me that our focus can be combined with strength. The campfire circles under the stars, sending flames flying high into the dark night. Singing *Kumbaya my Lord*, someone is crying with the light of fire just enough to see sparkling teardrops falling down each other's faces.

I found myself looking up at the cloudless ceiling facing sleep straight on. A struggle ensued as the thoughts seemingly grew louder but it was instead a racing heartbeat without words, it was silent but noisy. It grabbed my attention, I felt more awake. I was facing the steep cliff of jumping off into dreams, conundrum, the quandary of in the dark while lying still. It was an athletic summmersault without moving, a skill we can all do in our sleep. A way into the mystery, into the dark, through the veil without even looking.

It's warp speed, but you sink in, soak it up, become a sponge. We are all experts at it. We just don't know the very mechanics of it, and think it is a process, a step-by-step logical method, but it isn't. Something is organizing life. We need do nothing, only melt into the sky of dreams. The universe does the rest. The more we surrender to life, the more she puts us in charge. It's a two-way street.

Leave it alone. LIVE LIFE. Step out of its way. Travel light, share the light, be the light.

The wind stopped. It ceased. The day had resumed into peace, the peace of night, yet the world kept spinning. The stars kept shining. Months went by singing mantras.

Lightning Cloud

Our mother's hand would come in, quietly, gently, in the dark, making soft circles, barely touching my skin, my face, my forehead, then walk off without a sound. I didn't have to see her bleeding hands. I felt safe now to dive in. Make a move. A move into heaven. The heaven of dreams.

Then a light would invite itself into the south side window and gracefully make its way in a slow-motion tip toeing around my room, calibrating itself to investigate while going over my turtles' bowl, which were continually dying of soft shell, it seemed to stop, to be looking in, and then curtail past my chalk board of pretend school, fill in the blank sentences, and exit over my head, out the window.

I wondered how a car going parallel to our house can be creating this circular light, taking corners while going straight by. It was a turning point. It's not about the corner, but about embracing, the surround sound of existence all around us. The curve of life, the spiral. Alive. We walk through. Conscious or unconscious, when one is shocked awake, as in a death, all the unconscious that ever was, is also lit up, all at once, dissipates.

It's a match, a flame of peace. 'Relax, I got this,' says the universe as in a dream which you can't remember. You can't remember the whole thing, but you have just a piece, just a part of it. I capture this one image and hold onto it, keep focused on it, take time with it, suddenly in a vivid effulgence the whole dream, in a lightning flash, not from beginning or end, develops instantly, in layers all at once.

Otherwise, I was going down the hall in my mother's fleece braided coat with another passed over turtle in its crinkled up tin foil casket in one hand and my cedar wood recorder, in the other, passing the kitchen while my mother was on the phone with the curled-up cord over to the pot of boiling water at the stove for another night of spaghetti, then down the long looking back stairwell to outside, while the hem of the coat picks up the last dandelion puffs across the lawn, to the edge of the woods where the path lay a spot to brush over the sand and dig a new home for turtle number, of which I had lost count. I played my recorder. Its cedar smell filled the forest.

I unburied a turtle once, just to see in. It was ashes. I thought did I open it up into the past or did I open it up to the future? I did not know. It was in tin foil. Aluminum is not a conductor. Perhaps, I let its spirit free.

Ear infections plagued me back then, subsequent perhaps from handling the turtles, of which back then, no one knew of the possible salmonella. Subsequently, after the third consecutive doctor's visit, I had to have my tonsils and adenoid out. They grew back.

Subsequently, I found when I coughed into my pillow, a spark of lightning would come out of my mouth like static electricity in a fork-like uneven pattern. My pillow was filled with down feathers—a cloud for my head. Once my earaches were gone and no more cough, I would then cough on purpose to create the spark of light that looked like tree branches. I wanted to give the bird feathers invisible inside my pillow, another way of landing in trees. To free them once again into flight, I dreamed.

It was so much fun in the night and a very quiet thing to do, no one knew the magic that can be done alone, together in the dark, three to a room. The static lightning emanating from my tongue was so silent no one could hear. A private light show of excitement, an inner chemistry was clear.

Subsequently, my first scientific project in sixth grade was on lightning, only four pages.

Christine Manke did trees, it was 93 pages. I wondered if she knew that lightning and trees have the same pattern.

It was a science project to be presented before the class. Our teacher, Ms. Roberts, pointed out my mistake in front of everyone. She told me to look at the spelling while I stood in front of the class. I spelled Lightning, Lighting, without putting in the extra n after the t. This was so embarrassing, but instead, I had to say to myself, '*There is a reason for this crack in your armor, Brya, be still, you will need this moment later to add to your story. The story of you.*'

However, the most amazing thing I learned from Ms. Roberts was 'stream of consciousness' writing. I learned to write endlessly, to merge, to blend, to create the core of expression, the alphabet, the language of light. Consequently, in many composition notebooks, that is all I was writing, the same thing, repeatedly, God is Love, but in as many forms of writing as possible. We exchange air with the trees. They give us wood for shelter and houses, and we give them their words through our books. Nothing is ours. It's all intertwined. If only we could use the billions of leaves that fall each autumn from the forest for paper and packing materials, instead of the entire tree.

Mayril kept me home from school sixty days a year to clean, cook, dress and shop with the littler ones, while she lay exhausted on the couch with a Coca Cola by her side. The phone would ring, and I would hear her saying to my teacher, "Mrs. Talmadge, Brya is not missing anything; life is not learned in a book." But later, in college, I did not miss a single day. Even the first day, starting the semester in January, was a snowstorm, two feet deep. I still got there. I was the only fool doing this, no one was on the road for miles in any direction.

One time, staying absent from school, my mother had sent me to shop, and I had bought so many things for the family that the bags ripped while trying to walk down North Brookvale towards home. The items all fell out all over the sidewalk. Subsequently, cars were stopping to ask if I needed a ride, but I had to say no to them because they were strangers, then they would say, but we are your neighbor, but I said no, again, "I can do this", because only their car looked a bit familiar, I had never really met them.

I would then just write my own excuse to get back into school. Learning Mayil's penmanship exactly to the T. I felt like I turned into her, she turned into me. I didn't know which one was real.

In the forest were my friends. The Elders. I swung on my swing talking to the trees. She started this, my mom, she spoke to trees like they were family, like she was talking to me. Some were my grandparents' aunts and uncles. Until I met a walking stick that surprised me on a branch.

Camouflaged, its green grass body, its sticklike legs, it felt like I had found me. There in a large tree hidden in with all the other real branches, just like me, there, in a large family, invisible. Just a number. Just another turtle's death. Just like how many children are being born we might lose count someday forcing us to use our number instead of our name. I loved the number three, however, the trinity, that was me, third in line. That triangle of mother and father pointing up into the mystery, the finger of God, to super consciousness, the holy ghost.

It was fun at birthday parties to take the balloon and rub it on our heads so that the hair would charge the electrical static enough to stick it to the ceiling.

Otherwise, we were driving once a year to upper New York State, to Syracuse, visiting the relatives on DeRuyter Lake. I saw it all ahead; the six-hour trek and the distorted image of my face in the chrome backseat ashtray, reflecting my face like a Picasso. The silos of peeling red paint were flowing out with grain. Rain clouds could be seen far off as blurred gray fog settling on the hills in the distance.

I learned to get the outside door seat or both shoulders would become a pillow. I wouldn't fall asleep, but my arms would go into tingling but for a good reason, for the greater good, the family.

After jutting past treetops, rooftops of every shade from black to white, blurring in and out of view, and telephone poles creating a silent staccato, and the perpetual bumps in the road hitting the highway holes, creating a rhythm. I learned to get my grounding latching on the first star of twilight. My only recourse remaining for some much-needed balance and not to get dizzy with the backseat bumping blues, into distorted images in the chrome ashtrays, as tunes of static playing up front.

I was staring at the star. Holding it in my focus at every twist and turn. Keeping an eye. Suddenly, the star I was staring into reversed its light and shone back something that filled me instantly within. I felt I was disclosed of life's purpose, without a single word being said. It moves me today and keeps going. It never stopped doing this. No one knew. I did not disclose it because it was beyond words, it was beyond what we know any words could ever convey, truth seemed to be the only thing real.

I felt a euphoria that seemed to be more than an emotion, it felt like the technology of life itself had just given me full knowledge of the theory of everything, without a single word, and the highest intelligence is emotion, a wave, a motion moving higher feelings, deeper, higher, more.

Otherwise, we were all getting ready for school without any help, it was a predictable chaotic event, but no one bumped into each other, and everyone was ready at the same time standing in front of the screen door to get out. Mayril was chanting her 'hurry up' syndrome again, without it doing anything, just a background clock clicking in her own projected extensions into our little lives. Then she would rush us, her small city of offspring, into the woody station wagon with the giant flower painted on it, to go backward out the sandy driveway, turning around in the road to face down to go to Norton school at the bottom of the hill on Brookvale.

We would all pile out to go into a square room with square desks and a green rectangular chalkboard to do carry-over math. I was waiting for the lessons to start. They never did. I wanted to learn something significant like how a bunch of kids can get ready perfectly without a single word. There was order in chaos, there was method in the madness, was my first lesson in life. Something was organizing all of matter.

I wanted to learn about synchronicity because I believed it could change the world and save mankind to find this instant knowing of God in every breath. In all things around us and the instant connection and communication thereof and therein.

Life has a mind all its own, it's in the air, its synchronicity. We breathe it in. Every breath, every thought reaches everywhere, even to other galaxies we impact, we exist.

I just thought, everyone knows this, right? No, I felt no one did, only me, alone together. They say a one child family is so lonely, but the same can be amplified in a large family, without significance lonelier.

Otherwise, I was stacking my 45 MGM RCA vinyl up in piles with the portable diamond needle record player to dance in Sally's basement each day after school, to Elvis, Dione Warwick, the Supremes or over at Candy Wood's, to listen to Homeward Bound by Simon and Garfunkel, 100 times, while lying on her horse barn roof, catching the sun, and getting too hot up there, climbing fast back down.

Black soul came in from Mo Town records and the world would never be the same. The soul of love and spirit, of depth and global healing could be heard from the voices with the most powerful meanings. From here in U.S.A., out to the whole planet. The king of rock and roll was the great James Brown and to me Mr. Satchmo with 'What a wonderful world', Marvin Gaye, 'What's Going On'. We did the mash potato, the twist, the jerk. The limbo. At recess everyone played dodge ball and triple jump rope together. Once, our teachers let us have a dance outside, I played *Secret Agent Man* on my portable.

It was the day of the Black Panthers and Angela Davis, Martin Luther King and speeches about harmony in humanity and uplifting mankind, and how this was our chance. The voices were from the heart.

We moved to the bottom of the hill, to 360 Brooksvale Road, to the original farmhouse in the neighborhood. 360 had 27 windows and a wraparound porch with edible, trumpet honeysuckle bushes, at each pillar. We would pull the stamen out from the center of the petal to drink the drop of glistening elixir.

There was a two-level barn and a two-car garage with a very old perennial rhubarb garden. We made forked piecrust baked twice, once without the filling then again adding the filling. We pinched the edges down into a scalloped pattern circling around the circumference.

Otherwise, my mom and I would go to the clock shop on Whalley Avenue in Hamden to visit our grandfather's fine jewelry store, Fowlers. We parked in the back by the swinging bridge over the reservoir's river. I would be running up the slanted cement wall to meet her there then jump down, and in, as she opens the door. There were clock chimes ringing off the wall. Coo coos of every whistle, of every unique figurine bird. I met Ruth, the only female watchmaker in the line-up of three men, with the flashlight head band, as she turned smiling. I just know that if time never stops, then how can there be any time at all.

I just know that if space goes on forever then how can there be any place to come to, what will give this place, we are in, any difference from forming 8 billion miles away, why here, how can this be where we are? If space goes on forever, what will give a certain somewhere to come to? Could it be that no matter where we go in space, there we are, we come back to ourselves and there is no place that we are not, in other words, worlds…we, our consciousness, takes up all space, and space is not a distance, it is not a place, it is a being, it is I am that I am; alchemized.

I was put on task right away, as soon as I got there, to do the bows in the hallway, with the V slicer apparatus. The handle rotated, cranking the ribbon eight times around then an arm came down to cut a v shape at the center of the loops, making two sides. One piece of thin ribbon was cut to tie them together, then with the tips of my fingers I found the inner loop and pulled out each one, individually out, starting from the inner one, creating a blossoming flower, then proceeded by dropping it into the box below. It was a for a gift, to be forever present to opening it and not knowing what is inside, joyful happiness, of embracing the mystery, the mystery of in all of life. Because even though it is a mystery, we can be fully present to it and no box can ever contain us.

In 1970, the Bonsignore daughter, Jaye, was initiating people into Transcendental Meditation that Guru Maharishi founded. She gave me my first real mantra, all to myself. She whispered it into my left ear, Ieeme.

After my first meditation, which lasted 15 minutes, we all talked afterward to go over what we experienced. When it was my turn, I said I felt empty, but filled with peace, and added that the sound of a truck going by the house, up the hill passing by out front, grabbed my attention, but instead of it sounding too loud and not liking its interruption, I felt no judgment, not attaching to the sound but just allowing, just letting it to pass by. Nothing in the way. Like the mantra I was given, Jaye taught us is to be used when you want, as needed, if you desire, always present to the potential and not the goal or outcome. The measure but not the measurement. The mantra, but not a word, I am attaching a thing to an object from, a sound, but like a bubble in the ocean, like the breath, a wave, thoughts float, hearts beat. I was able to witness thinking as just a function of the whole body, freed.

This time, the repeated word would be natural, never forced for whenever one feels moved to do so, no real rules. Like the breath in and out, the tides the ocean waves, consciousness surfaces, like bubbles, the mind begins to open, the heart softens. This was my first mantra beyond my Mantra Mother Mayril.

"Go ahead," Eileen said from outside, under my window on the first floor. "I'll catch it, don't worry," she assured me. So, I did. I dropped the doll out the second-story window and it fumbled right through her fingers, shattering into the grass.

"Oh no," I said, "my mother is going to kill you," I yelled down to her, leaning over outside my window. The doll's head was made of fine porcelain china. I showed Mayril and she was not upset at all. We had to get the glass out of the grass wearing thick rubber gloves.

No sooner moving from 1137 Long Hill Road to 360 Brookvale we had to move again, to 977 North Pleasant Street in Amherst, 80 miles north.

Bryce had opened his own branch of the family jewelry stores up there in Amherst and off we went, stuffed like sardines, elbow to elbow in the back seats, an hour and a half north, up interstate 91. Mayril and Bryce had found a house but someone else bid higher, so we had to take a tour of a different one, at 977, which was much smaller, and move in, in time for school, all seven of us, hurried up.

When we got there, some siblings were sleeping, with their heads on the shoulder of the one next to them, like dominoes cascading. I had someone's elbow sticking into my ribs, keeping me awake. We got off at exit 19 ramp and turned immediately right onto route 9 east toward Amherst for 7 more miles.

At the apex of the Calvin Coolidge bridge, you could see the Mt. Holyoke Range. Bryce pointed out its 1100-foot unusual east-to-west orientation. Most mountains go north to south. The riverbank trees had clutching, entangled roots above the ground, as the water washes away, tipping out over to reflective glass mirrored images some ready to fall in, slowly surrendering, with nothing in the way.

We could see the stoic Skinner House sitting solo against the contiguous contours of its Seven Sister peaks over to our right. A path was evident going up its cliff edges to reach the top. It was the rail trail where the trolley once carrying thousands of visitors had left its mark, a scar through the face of the mountain remaining and looking like a ladder. Panoramic views were afforded to those that reached the top, all the way up to the Skinner House. Scenic views encompassing Mount Monadnock in New Hampshire, my dad kept telling us more.

The Windsor locks dam would shut down, allowing for the oxen to pull the tourist boats through the Oxbow to get over to the trolley. This part of the river would empty. Sixty feet below, at the apex of the bridge was a current of jetties still spinning an archival history. Back from the era the Algonquin used to make their fishing traps, lining them with rocks, still surfacing. Once the boats with passengers were pulled through, and the dam released, the river rushed back in like a tidal wave, thus meaning Connecticut in Algonquin.

The seven of us, some half asleep, looking out over the highest point of the bridge seeing the Mt. Holyoke range with Skinner House standing solo against a single cloud against the blue sky and tall pillars. This is a historic landmark with a unique geological configuration. A river meandering through, picturesque.

Then Bryce added that this area in the Pioneer Valley had 5 colleges with 25 thousand students all in a 20-mile radius. We then went by the just constructed 28 story, tallest library in the world, at the time, at UMass, before turning into the driveway of our house, at 977. Arriving to our destination at North Pleasant Street the 7 siblings piled out. We were all wobbling side to side, as the circulation was flooded back in, needing walkers. We took the tour of the house, and immediately turned back.

When we got back to Cheshire and pulled into the driveway, I could hear the phone ringing off the wall from inside the porch screen door to the kitchen. Running in to answer it in time, the screen door slammed shut behind me.

"Did you hear?" Laurie asked. "Eileen died; she was hit by a car Friday night."

"Oh no," I said, and could not stop repeating it, no, no, no, in complete shocked disbelief.

Then it happened: my first death, a human and not a turtle. Eileen died and was freed while I died inside, still alive. A juxtaposition, I just had to get to the bottom of, so I could find freedom again. So, I could have back my earthly wings.

How is it that she is happy and dies into light, while I am here and living in the sun, but entirely in the dark now? How is this fair, how can this be? She went into the dark, but really into the light of heaven and filled with gods light, while I am here in the bright sun, in the dark.

Lined up under the arched spacious church ceilings, we all sat at the funeral, and voices were heard from the back, some still making fun of her, perhaps, rising, echoed off and back down, to all of us, sitting in pain, broken, yet, totally open hearted. This is the epitome of love in reverse. A crescendo.

Three months later, after the wake, the funeral services and time to move permanently to Amherst, Carol called me to come see her. When I get there, I see I am being motioned by a person at the front door to wait a moment while the Dobermans are escorted around to the back yard. Then the woman waves me in. It's a spacious house, with sparce furniture that seemed stylishly stoic and simple, yet strong and elegant, in a distinct sense of grandeur and grace, this abode had such style. It was so good to finally speak to Carol. I had been waiting, because she was the last one with my friend.

I really wanted to know if my friend had said anything about me before she passed over. I just really felt anguished, not being able to apologize and acknowledge the friendship goes both ways with Eileen. She always looked up to me for befriending her, while others calling her names. I wanted to say to her, what I never got a chance to say, how I looked up to her, too.

The last time I was with Eileen flashed before me. The doll slipping through her hands; the doll's head made of porcelain, disappearing into the grass.

My mother let me know that the cause of death had been a head injury. Deep guilt consumed my entire being, as if I caused it, as if my words, that she would die for breaking the doll, came true, was prophetic, linked in even deeper, with this unresolved reality, face to face into the tide of a broken heart, love and pain collide.

I left for Amherst, the following day. It was June of 1971. Only one thing remained, only one thing I took with me and that was Eileen's laughter, her voice, her joy. I did not know, going over the Calvin Coolidge bridge again, that I was going forward from a place that was erased, and buried. I was otherwise an empty shell. At seemingly random times and without questioning it, the laughter would resurface. A thread of light, as if she were still here, right beside me, like a tape recording, I could hear, not inside, not a memory but audibly real. I got used to it and never questioned it. I brought her with me. She and I were closer than ever, in spirit, for now it was 24/7. Travel free in time and instant. The laughter was a thread of light, the only thing real, my strength, my medicine. Her love resided in a stillness within me, intrinsically, invisible strength.

Here we go again, with seven in tow and a trailer behind going over the bridge to Amherst, for the third time. The scene itself is filled with its unique history. The meandering, wide, river cutting through a notch in the mountain, the jetties below, the Skinner House above. I prayed to the openness of the sky, to find me. I was going from a past that was erased, to a future unknown.

I felt like my life was spinning, like the jetties, going nowhere fast. Stuck. Like a hamster wheel, turning around and around, again and again. This cyclic earth pattern made me realize the turtles' deaths were a premier, a training, for what it is like to have a human death stuck inside you, with so much pain, I knew it had a purpose. I had to wait, in faith, trusting the deeper meaning, the higher emotional intelligence I did not see, yet.

Moving to Amherst, I thought, this place is for me. I fit in. The unusual orientation of the mountain, 5 colleges condensed into one area, the tallest library in the world, with me, a one of a kind, named Brya.

Sophia at Sirius

I would meet the first person in Amherst at the Sirius Bookstore, her name Sophia, whom, I would never actually physically meet but would become a thread through my life, weaved in and slowly revealed from the wisdom of the mystery of life when looking back. The proprietor of the bookstore was an astrologer. I would walk the isles of esoteric books to read Alice Bailey, Alan Watts, Madam Blavatsky, Zen, Taoism, Buddhism and Hinduism books. It was a shop with subjects that, like me, were strange but highly intelligent, interesting, alluring. They were themes about something below the surface, behind the physical, the unseen to me was more real than the real, the things that never die, energy, light, virtues.

Sophia, an archetypal model, or conceptual belief was being defined to a customer. Listening intently, moving closer and closer to the front isles. He kept saying what the word meant, adding life to Sophia and this word archetypal, both which started following me throughout my life, as you will see, or was I following it?

I had gotten my yoga books and *I Ching* there. I remember running all the way home to investigate in every single dictionary we had in our 3 story house, to further find out more about archetype. We had five. But none of them said enough. They all left me still wondering what the meaning of an archetype is. The description of life itself can never be in a single word, except the wordless energy love.

So now I have Eileen that I can't see but with me 24/7, and in comes this word, this word that thrills my soul, archetype. I felt each description in each dictionary that they all were leaving something out. This word could not be contained, defined, and even trying seemed blasphemous in some way. I could not pin it down, and neither could they. It was an open question insatiable, stuck in my mind.

How can a word be inclusive of explaining life? The mystery of life needs to always stay unknown, its mere energy, its potential, its soil of fertile ground and forever dirt of rich possibilities can't be put in a box, only seeds. Or life would die. Life would stop, it would freeze into the box of the mind to the chains of thought. For life is the very essence of there is no point to it, but that does not stop us from appearing as a point, an atom, Adam. All the past and all the future is always right here. All at once, blossoming.

From the depths of the earth, from in the beginning, was the dark. The dark gets a bad name, but it is associated with our unconscious shadow but even in the light of day we can have a shadow, the soul. The truth of the dark, being space, being open, being free, is that it's truth that encompasses both the light and dark so we can be in existence. In the dark is the greatest light. The white light of heaven has all colors to the spectrum, and the other side, of the eternal 8th symbol we can see, duality, the eyes recycle the word the reflection, the light we see, this as truth behind everything, is the dark containing all colors, with white the absence of color. This template. This blossoming LIFE form has no past or future, for its creative, an art.

The Sirius Bookstore proprietor continued to explain all about Sophia. Sophia, he was saying, stands for wisdom, she is the alpha and the omega, she comes to earth to help people knowing she will suffer along with them but can always leave when she wants to. Sophia came before God brought light. God says and, in the void, I create the stars and heaven. The dark, the deep the fertile was the material genesis was born from. The mystery is pointless but that doesn't mean it doesn't have a point. The point of fertility, the goddess, of the womb, the deep, to propagation. Just like our family, so fertile. I felt I vicariously knew all about the template of life, the template of duplication.

The dark, the deep the emotion, the memory, the significance comes from out of the dark, out of the mystery. If we knew what the mystery was, we could not have open space, space to grow, space to be. In the dark, the womb, the room, the woman, is all unity of knowledge. It is the spiral of life, once a circle embracing, giving birth, through the tunnel. The brokenness of life makes us all perfectly imperfect. The light gets into us through our compassion, our feelings, our openness. Emotions are cleared, opened, when we allow this growth. Feel the pain openly and free the actual attachments but keep its fuel, its power, its wisdom. For only making memories imbibed with love.

The universe absorbs our emotions when we talk about them, share them, release them often, allowing the mystery to do her job, dissipate, and balance. If we neglect, shy away or do not free them they built up, and if someone else tries to share theirs, then one holds back, then the other emotions from the partner, spill out more for ultimate importance than the other person closes off more, escalating the imbalance, to trust, discuss, use words, let thoughts be linked completely to your heart, becomes evaded. The art of sharing emotions through compassionate listening through sacred space with a partner once a week, perhaps even at a set designated time, works wonders.

On one occasion, I went into a magic shop that had opened recently behind our jewelry next to the Bangs Community Center Boltwalk. It was a small shop with very little elbow room with only two tall and narrow display cases. I went inside and asked the owner if he believes in real magic. He took out some cards and placed them on the top of the display cases wooden framed countertop and splayed them out like a fan face-down. He said in a doubtful way, thinking someone would have the audacity to challenge his new jewelry store intentions, to someone playing pretend to know real magic; it was furthering doubt in the air.

I sensed it could affect the outcome, his negativity, change the magic, for it is my positive that does it. How much influence someone else has, I did not know, but if it does not work out, then I can never point out to them that it was their own block that made sure to stop the magic, or I call it, CHI of Life Force because it is our natural state, alpha, bliss, magic of light. Because how do we prove the art of faith, the art of dying to our own limiting beliefs? Some customers walked in and stepped over behind me to see what was going on. He called out for me to find the queen of hearts, then I turned it over. His jaw dropped but the people inside said it was a setup, a show, as I was walking out, and they did not believe it. *Oh well*, I thought, *I am not here to convince others of the underlying connection to all things communicating with us.*

However, subsequently, I came down with anorexia nervosa. Reaching below 70 pounds and three months without any food. When I went out to dinner with family, I would chew and then put the foot into a napkin, then into my purse. I felt fat looking in the mirror even though I saw skinny as a rail. I was close to death if I kept up this charade and to be hospitalized soon. Mayril, pointing her finger in my face told me flat out, you will die if you don't start eating. My Mantra Mother Mayril knew best how to scare me to death, while fully alive.

It worked; the next day I was eating. Joy went with me. Eileen's laughter followed me. It was invisible, yet it was real like an anchor, and had given me the light I needed to go on. A gift from Eileen from the other side, until I got my life back, my emotional connections returned for myself, who I am and what I feel came to life and Eileen's giggle I had heard out of nowhere, had taught me how to still stay in a connection with the deceased, even if just a thread, a mere string, it is still music, it is still a song in the space of time, a way to that connects to otherworldly, through sound. Even at the famous Coral Castle in Florida he could move megalithic stones, alone, through the gravity release of a certain frequency. Through a vibration and using 16 magnets, wheel of mystery. Just like the hieroglyphs on the pyramids that look like a harp but are sound wave instruments that assist in levitating the rocks.

The Nile River has been found to be 30,000 years old, not 10,000 as originally thought because this river is now 9 miles away. The river used to flow around or under the great pyramid of Giza. It would take 30 thousand years for a river to move that distance away.

We need to reverse the love of power with the power of love, said Jimi Hendrix, tuning to 432 hertz, not 440.

Paul Oppenheimer was two grades above me. He was in the 11th grade. I was invited to his house in Pelham for dinner. He said his family was from a long line of scientists and that a distant relative was the one to discover an amazing measurement of space. He asked me if I had ever heard of it. I said, "no, what is it," curiously.

Paul said that, even though an object is being sent out in a straight measured line, it is still curving. All space curves. This was music to my ears. Years of headlights coming in my window and circling my room flashed before me.

Then I did the first Natal Astrological chart outside mine, outside each one in the metropolis family. I constructed one of my brother's friend, Christie. I had been learning my own natal chart, vicariously, backward, each year. Each year I would have an astrologer with a different zodiac sign decipher my birth chart. In this way, I could see if they interpreted my chart scientifically, with some set framework, or if it was purely subjective information.

The Gemini astrologer told me a little bit about each aspect, the Scorpio astrologer, went deeper into centering on my Saturn in Scorpio. Then a Sagittarius astrologer, focused mainly on my Sagittarius North Node, which is the purpose of life from the orbital axis of the moon and the sun cross. My findings concluded, using myself as a study guide, how each interpreter gave me the same basics and had the same information just emphasized my chart according to their own sign.

I was learning two things at once, my own chart, and the behaviors and mind structures of each sign while interpreting my chart, simultaneously. I learned I had four fire signs, three air, three water and zero earth in my chart. Perhaps that is why I always want to fly. I always want to study the highest wisdom. I guess I am lucky to be writing this book, finding me, into the visible, with a material book, is an earth driven objective, set in stone, step by step, a marriage to procedural commerce.

I learned Neptune rules spiritual, dreams, illusions and compassion and that Neptune at my time of birth sits right on my equator line. Each one said that I am highly idealistic, and perhaps would lead a life in solitude. It was consistent, my nature attributes, and characteristics all geared by the mystic, behind the veil qualities of soul. My findings for Christie, with the bright blue eyes and wavey blond hair, was an altruistic leader, with many aquarian planets, a true humanitarian.

Here, at 977 Amherst, was a hill behind the house. I would sit up at the hill at sunset and listen to the busy town below slowly stop there hammering and other activities as the sun was setting the peoples activities, the sounds the kids playing the traffic slowed was like a musical score, diminuendo in unison with the suns final colorful glow all around us. I would sit up here on the hill, with the swaying tall corn stalks and hear their stalks rubbing up against each other as they swayed gently in the breeze standing tall beside me, and then learning later that in Indian lore humans come from corn.

At massage school, in 2003, we were given a large flat bowl of watered-down cornmeal and told to massage it. We found that the corn held a memory. If we switched the petrissage stroke pattern the paste would resist. But when we continued with the same strokes, the mixture was open to it and made a wake along with the movement of the hand, working together. Indicating the importance of starting slow, and light so the body acclimates.

In twelfth grade, my friend from Conway, CT., visited with his friends after attending a 9-year-old guru initiation called The Knowledge. They said there were four secrets to inner light, inner music, inner nectar, and inner bliss.

When they left, I immediately ran up to my attic to try this. It had a pyramid 45-degree angled ceiling, I didn't have the mantra for this meditation. Dale had told me that they could not tell me the mantra because I would have to get that from the guru in person, through an initiation. I opened my eyes back up and reached over to my bookshelf. The book I grabbed was a Hinduism Tiger Eye book. Opening the 240-page paperback, which I read so much the cover was coming off, I turned to the one page in the whole book that had mantras on it and saw 'om pad me hum hui wei'.

I closed my eyes and focused on the space that they showed me, the space between the eyes on the forehead, and started chanting the mantra. Suddenly, I felt something come into the room. It was a static electric kind of energy you feel after a lightning storm, it had an exotic, spontaneous, sensual sensation of a keen awareness of the physical, an invisible primal life force, very conscious, very sparkly. It was in each corner of the room, as it was also fully occupying and stimulating my cells of my body into a source life energy, but nothing was there but me, and it felt lizard like, or primal, with a stark awareness of life itself on steroids, tingling power.

I felt something moving up my spine. I opened my eyes to see if I had moved in any way as I was sitting still in a lotus sutra. I was still in the same spot, so I closed my eyes again starting the om mantra back up. As soon as I did, a bolt of light struck through me. I turned into a euphoric state of mind instantly, like lightning I was all lit up. The sensation was a totality of bliss. Enough to fill the whole universe. The boundaries of my skin were invisible. A stream of white-water rapids was flowing down through me, terraced, cascading. The vision and the euphoria were the same source in motion together.

My eyes, the vision, and my body, all one. I was whole and inclusively authenticated by this vision, inseparable. It felt like the earth had swallowed me. It felt like all visions, all of nature, all of life, was this ignited bright light of colors and music. Like entering the Garden of Eden must be. This river, with rapids, was forever a flow, a birth, rebirthing, I could see the bright white light, and so vivid was a chorus that was linked into this state of mind, of such melodic beauty never heard before on this planet in this life in this body and then the taste of the river; was a taste of sweet heaven a food, a fuel, an essence that I was drinking and it was beyond any food on any corner store or gourmet grocery, could offer in any country could I ever discover here on the earth on this planet. Heaven on earth, had come here. Heaven is within you and me.

I said, '*why did I see a straight ray of light that had no boundaries?*' Years later, I realized it was because light is not a ray, it is a circle. I felt that the light I had seen went all the way to infinity and back in one second. Thus, creating a circle, thus, even though I have a linear body, the light was not going in a ray through me, this was my misconception, it seemed this way, but on deeper study, light is always a circle and the diameter of the circle, at the midpoint is the figure for the sound of light, the spot, the point, otherwise light is always fully around us. The Quantum Slit experiment with the two holes that light passes through does not take this into account. That is why I could see all the way around, from the beginning of my life, to the end, I have already lived, or at least envisioned and already been through all this, the light showed me my whole film, and because I sit not yet at the end, then it will be interpreted as a circle, by a linear mind, limitation, will never see.

For three days a current of, 'I need do nothing,' kept me in the palm of God, of source's, of the Christ's healing hands. Every cell was aligning in my body, like dominoes, each day, a completeness forming. I could see that everyone was looking down, focused on a task, conditioned in their minds, blinded to the real thing, the real source of all this flowing through us.

I could see that if only we woke up, if we, so to speak, look up, if we feel all our living feelings then we could be fully charged and we have a complete synchronicity with God in us now, not tomorrow or later, not waiting, not at the end, not at the illusion of death and or dying. This current lasted in full force each atom in my body attuned, magnetized like when we go into an MRI, and the image forms after all atoms are at the same point, then dropped away from the source, photos. The atoms had a mind of their own. I could look down and be fully dressed, meaning what I did had zero-point effort in the face of God, in the hands, an innocence, I was living in its light. I was doing what we are all here to do, being completely amazed at where we are and be in complete thankfulness and praise of love in action, being in form, yet freedom.

Running the River Rocks

There I was running without looking down, my feet had eyes of their own and I learned our bodies have a mind of their own and a rock, a tree has a mind of its own and we share a being, a mind, a memory that is everywhere and singular all at once; it's holographic.

Myriah invited my brother, Bryce, Jr., for a picnic in Charlemont; she lived in an A-frame and had a recently tilled garden next to her picnic table. The night before I had happened to watch a Native Indian documentary about making rain. I asked Myriah if it was okay to try the dancing I saw on TV the night before, that brings the dust up, meets with moisture and makes it rain. Myriah said to go ahead, that she had not planted anything in the garden yet.

My feet sank into the soil. I started to pretend an Indian voice with guttural sounds in a rhythmic cadence. Suddenly, a real melody took over in me. I had become a channel, a vessel, empty and free enough to allow this somehow. I danced and felt an electrical charge coming up through my feet, and then a cloud, one single cloud, on a cloudless day appeared overhead. It came right over the picnic table and made everyone scramble back into Myriah's A-frame, grabbing the food and brand-new stereo speakers off the table.

I had learned the night before on a TV documentary about Indians making it rain. That the Indians make it rain when sand, dust rising, comingles with moisture, a theory seemed now so true. Instead of my experiment being fruitful others were not happy about getting all wet, out of nowhere.

A sample of synchronicity started happening while in college and working at a fabric outlet, when just the night before I had studied the famous actress Sarah Bernhardt's palm. Then less than 24 hours later the mom with her daughter was a student at UMass. I saw stars, the same kind of ones in Bernhardt's, in the same place, at each pad directly under each finger. I said, "You are majoring in art or theater." It was correct. She said yes. It was the first and last hand I ever saw of stars being featured so vividly.

Then I saw on the palm of another student from UMass a big x at the start of the birth line. I said, "Oh look, something happened at your birth."

He said, "Wow, yes, my mom was 17 at my birth and was paralyzed because I was ten pounds." This was showing right on his hand, in the lines on the palm.

I can only ascertain that once an inner eye is opened that all studies, astrology, palmistry, numerology that we analyze, go to the same place, all open the DNA patterns and visions therein into a naked light.

Then someone came over to me putting his hand out, palm face up, and I said, "You should not even be here, your lifeline stops cold at around 18 years old." He looked at his palm, and then looked at me, lifting his bangs. His forehead had a major scar. He said he had been in a car crash two years before and was pronounced dead and then came back after resuscitation. A faint line had started up again, looking closer.

I bought a tarot deck with 78 cards. The higher arcana is 22 court cards, and the lower deck is 56. 22 represents the Hebrew language alphabet. Our bodies are created by actual sound waves, the I am, the OM, the word. The instructions mention to either take the first card out that best relates to the querant, the seeker, named the significator. I could take out the queen of cups, or wands, or swords but would shuffle and forget this first step, an option really, recommended but not set in stone.

I would come home every day after school, going straight up to the attic and shuffle, asking important question. The question would be regarding school, or family, or feelings unclear inside me, and the very first card for every single time, for two straight weeks, was the High Priestess. I wished someone was there with me. I just knew, I was not alone. I just knew something was organizing all matter, and it was made of a deep compassionate all seeing light. Merging the home of our heart with the universal love from heaven.

Then my sister's boyfriend came up the attic's steep narrow stairs and asked to use the death card, which is a metaphor for transformation in the esoteric, metaphysical realms, the force of life, of constant change. Dennis wanted to paint the image on the card onto his motorcycle. He was a Scorpio, which rules Pluto, which rules the intensity of 'life and death' bonding, and undercurrents, recycling, sexuality and reproduction. It was very synchronic; he was looking for the one card out of 78 that represents his actual zodiac sign.

I never see death in a tarot reading, and if this card comes up, it is about changing something. Fear not the death card it does not represent a physical death, it is about, transformation of oneself, to a whole new level. I only need to change one thing and that one thing is everything. That's what Scorpios tend to do, instead of working on one thing to repair, they repair the whole thing. The Scorpio, recycling of energy, the deepest most meaningful focus, creative force of the soul.

The Scorpio and the eagle all in one representing the cycle of life. To find that center and not go to extremes is the role of the Scorpio. Use the energy that stands in-between for higher purposes, to take raw life force and develop it. As is the planet that is represented by Pluto, the planet of the souls' evolution. The planet, which was changed into a planetoid, and this planet rules just that, change. Of all the planets to morph, this one rule that energy exactly. Taking what little you may have, like me, and building a mountain. Finding inner resources. My Saturn which resides in the placement of Scorpio, deep research of the spiritual domain.

I handed him the transformation or death card. Dennis started down the stairs, my fan sparked and stopped. I said, "Wait a minute. I read that I am advised to keep all the cards always together, to never let one go too far away, that it is a book and needs to stay together."

This card implies but does not have to mean a physical death because death does not exist the way we think, and every second is death of trillions of cells. Scorpios go to the extremes. The eagle flying high with angels or the scorpion stinging itself. That space between the two represents potential, static space, the primal, elements of life and death, resources, recycling from the dirt, the hidden, the subconscious, to rise, to ascend. The energy of the Scorpio is simple, when they change something, they tend to want to change the whole thing, leading to their intensity when they could just do an over time, tweak.

It represents the eight house in astrology, the other, bonding, the resources, or empowerment.

He came back up and gave me back my card, handing it over to me; the fan started to go again.

I was alone together with a whole universe of angels above and only 14, not telling anyone about my perhaps imaginary life, by now never shared, kept in the dark, so much of myself is not really me but a channel that I open to. I can share subsequent this story with you. This blossoming of my soul. Perhaps all souls, a story about magic, a story about the focus of freedom from the very love of life in me, translates to an innocence never growing up, because exploring the essence of life is so fascinating, a spark of existence, one spark made all this.

Fear gripped me, caught in a lightning storm shortly thereafter. I tried to hide in someone's open garage because it was hitting the generator right above me and made a huge explosive bang, plus it was downpouring and I was walking home from school with still blocks to go, taking off my shoes.

I had to get out of this garage, I had not asked anyone. I got very brave and had no choice but to step back out into the storm. I felt the storm, and as I was communicating somehow it grew peaceful and it saw that I was there.

I kept walking in deep four-inch flood waters which was so crystal clear you could see the amplified blades of grass where my feet landing waving the grass back and forth from my walking, waving to and fro like they were under amplification, so much larger than life, was all the electricity around me, the surround sound from the storm's energy.

My father spent summers sitting in a low lounge chair at the edge of the ocean, soaking up the sun and sinking in the sand with the ebbing tides all summer at Rye Beach in New Hampshire.

Bryce had been burned by his sunbathing and it opened a scar he had on his thigh. His doctor had prescribed antibodies for three weeks and nothing. I gave him golden seal and it cleared up within minutes forming a purple scab immediately upon application.

I got to work at the family jewelry store through the Alps work study program. I worked a few days a week from noon onward. I did displays, sales, bookkeeping, light watch repairs, restringing pearls, engraving amulets, eating giant tuna grinders from the Hungry U, over in the next block, and counting the inventory of gold-leaf china tableware.

I signed up for the Amherst Regional High School Alps Program which allows their students to take college courses, as well as work study. I used it at the University of Massachusetts to enroll in a Hatha Yoga class which would take place on Harkness Road in Pelham.

The teacher said that yoga is better than brash exercising because it unifies the heart with movement through breath. He was exemplary in demonstrating the movements and the

7 counts of the intake breath and then the sutra movement, with the 7-count outbreath. But even more masterful was the way he conducted the actual session. The space was kept pure prana. Once we started, with the window ajar, the candle burning, there were no words. It was all done in pure silence. All 8 of us, for one hour. The room filled with an electrical charge we did not even know was exponentially increasing, was happening. I could walk home the three miles on a current of air that had no inclinations, no programming, no knowledge of any limiting beliefs, of anything to do with tire or exhaustion, I was in a boundless state of mind and body.

After a few weeks, I was walking home the 3 miles and found that with every step, it was like I was in a cloud and it was effortless, and nothing was counting anything, no tally in my body was taking place or ever would need to, nothing was taking away or using up. I had either stored so much energy that for the first time I felt physically powerful, or the breathwork had given me extra energy, I did not know if this could ever ware out and I could keep going walking hundreds of miles straight to God. This was boundless. No doubts in my mind, eternal, a flow of action and ease was love. It was life force, prana.

The concepts of the mind were not there, no judgments ruled me. I was clear. I had the eternal spark of existence in every step and even my back step, had this chi, this life force, in it. When I got home, I was even more wired, wired on harmony on life on a grace from God, or life's oneness, a purity of mind, body and heart, which no words can say, but that the body, the perfect reflection, is already saying just being alive, inclusive.

Hatha, he said, is the union between the lungs and movements of the body, working in unison. Seven breaths in and seven breaths out. The Hatha Yoga teacher was demonstrative before each class but then once it began, the body moved without words, instruction, and he was engaged fully in the postures as well right along with us. He furthered that most exercises stress the body, and work against the heart, but that this ancient yoga method was in harmony and after a few weeks I would feel a life force permeating.

I would get home with the same exact amount of energy, nothing changed. I had storage of the life force, sustained. The fuel of existence. Breath, but not just any breath, but conscious, on purpose breath in each move.

I also signed up for a work study extension to my business classes in speed dictation, typing and accounts receivable bookkeeping, with Ms. Shea. Ms. Shea gave me 100-wpm Gregg shorthand certification with a 75-wpm typing award. I remember hearing our great grandfather was a Morse Code operator at the railroad. Mayril would go with him at night on his shift and hold the vesta lamp for the train to see the stop. Her grandfather would take down the notes and tack it to a long thin iron rod to lift it up all the way to the conductor who would open his window and grab it for instructions about the rails.

This instant code and my 100 Gregg shorthand per-minute certification came easy perhaps from his genes, but even more so was the time playing a synthesizer, a song came out that I wrote which acquired very distinct shorts and longs, like a machine, coming through me and will someday have it deciphered to see if he was talking through me through the song in Morse code, is a message from the universe, from him, via sound.

In my social studies class, at the time, around 1974, back then, a Mr. Ames taught us about Zen Buddhism, if you try to get enlightened it will keep slipping away. Searching must stop. How do you stop something you are trying to go to? When you tell the mind to not think of something, your minds thinks about it more. That's the power of desire. Desire is good but it can also block us. We can get stuck there. It's an orange color in sound frequency. One must be still, be happily unhappy in the now, merging all thoughts and feelings, in openness and acceptance. Be in pure awareness, heartful, be just where you are, be it all, be the problems, be the pain, be open to life force, to change, to evolution. See from above.

This was helpful because the rush of purity had worn off and I was starting to think like a human and have judgments and limiting concepts blocking me in. I was bored by the mundane and feeling obsessed in getting back the spiritual wonder of the flowing light of euphoria with the taste of nectar beyond anything I would ever encounter to eat here, depressed. I had to learn that that experience is still and always with me and that if it was not for this mundane life, we have conditioned ourselves into and forgotten the truth of life, I would not be able to find it to go there to be it. Thus, desire prevail.

Both are equal in significance, the dark and the light work hand in hand. The negative is actually just a function, an anchor but we tend to associate the first feelings of it, because we do not have enough inner space and balance, or understanding, as pointing to our past, our wounds when in actually it is a powerful energy that can propel dreams off the ground, so to speak and another symbolism or analogy of the real meaning behind the functions of the body we tend to try and define and become ruled by instead of seeing its overall function for the souls expansion is 'la sustanifikque moelle', constant focus, constant goal, and easiest when one remains free of beliefs that chain us from the mind.

It was the innocence, being just like a child, that I connected with the creative light of life, but now trying to force it, grieve it, catch it, was only pushing it away. Like a bar of soap in the tub when you are trying to reach for it, and watching it floating further away.

If we have a lot of unresolved emotions, painful memories, we will associate this deeper energy as negative when it is earth, a real potential and deeply rewarding to encounter in self-love, a compassion which extends to all.

I was studying the *I Ching* and using the three coins each time to throw and receive my changing and unchanging 6 or 9 lines, to read and find out the wisdom of my questions to specific situations, to see what the essence of the problem translates and where they are coming from, of the natural world, the lakes, mountains, in combination with each other sparking a certain solution that derives from the essence in the natural world around us. I tapped into in so many ways of discovery once I learned through the 8 ball, Chinese bamboo sticks, palmistry, tarot, and *I Ching* from lines from the turtle bones found on the shores of the ocean. For me, it is what we take with us when we go. The full spectrum of things unseen is made visible, palpable, enriching, keeping my mind open, my heart engaged, to the nature of all things so stoic.

The *I Ching* has 64 hexagrams of the 6 changing lines. Their 5,000-year-old oracle from China. It was relating metaphors to the first daughter or the third son. It was the same structure as our family so vicariously I could see quick evidence of its accuracy in reading the auric field the accuracy, firsthand, and absorb the teaching how natures energies are significant representations of the soul and what's to come and why of the placements, the lines both changing and fixed.

I kept doing the yarrow sticks between my fingers or the three coins. The third daughter represents joyous lake. I wish someone could have been with me for all this. I was alone, together. It was a universal love, only God and I shared and Faith, my middle name, to believe in trust of a god from within, my constant aim.

In the *I Ching*, for example, is the joyous lake, symbolized by the third daughter, that would be me. The first and second daughter have other attributes they represent. In astrology, it is the tenth house, the house that represents achievements, like a mountain climber and it is depicted by the goat. These archetypes are not just outside us but develop within into codes of lower or higher spirit manifestation, qualities, such as in the innocent, the caregiver, the explorer. The *I Ching*, with its 64 codons, can place the joyous lake over the mountain hexagram, to produce a certain effect we see happening in a situation, or put the mountain over heaven, the creative, or the receptive, also, coming through with a certain characteristic that can explain in detail the action to be taken, the cautions and the exaltations.

For me, it is a symbiotic relationship between youthfulness and the universe. It's all alive. The Living Art of Art Thou, I am that I am, that life has presented as a canvas before us, morphing our love to ever blossom with this creative force, to higher conscious awareness as we feel the forever agelessness of our being, our soul on the inside, even at 100, young at heart.

Bryce Senior took off for Boliva watch-making school each week to NYC on the train. The older two had taken off to live permanently in CA. I started working at UMass in Continuing Ed which had merged temporarily due to renovations at Whitmore Administration Building with the Transfer Affairs Department.

There I did walk in, transferring and continuing students' questions, mail, matriculation applications for a few deans. It was 1978. I was watching over and helping with the family again, as my father received his watch repair certification and our mother had moved back to Connecticut without us, cooking and sweeping the kitchen floor.

The Sycamore Tree

It was the baby power fad in 1984. Every night before he was born, I would take my anatomy workbook with words in Latin to the tub to proceed to read it to him. The philosophy of baby power was that, as soon as a baby is born, we can start teaching languages, science, math, because they are like sponges and absorb quickly. I took it to heart and decided to start while he was still in utero. Each night I would soak my feet in the tub, from three levels of stairs to our apartment, much needed, into the relaxing warm water while also reading to him, knowing he could be listening and to start ahead, now. Later in his school, he took years of Latin and never studied and got straight A's.

I took it so far as to put speaker headphones, since my partner was a musician, onto my extended, expectant stomach. I took it so far as to play classical and rock and roll music to him, symbiotically. I thought it was interesting that I did the baby power fad before Elan's birth. I thought later, perhaps when he was born with what is called tongue tie, that being inside, beneath and in umbilical liquid, the words may have been muffled, and perhaps a subsequent adaptation mutation took place.

Elan's birth—taking 13 hours, on a Friday the 13th and weighing in at 7.6 pounds—happened when I was 28. After a few days in the hospital my partner drove up in our Volvo and we got in. I requested to pull over and I got out and held Elan up. We pulled into the Smith College campus and through the pillars to the giant 30 foot in circumference American Sycamore overlooking Paradise Pond.

I requested to pull over to get out into the fresh air… We stopped, I got out reaching into the back seat for my new born, Elan. We sat down on the marble bench, and I held him up into the streaming rays of sunlight landing at our feet. The midwife R.N. Linda LaPinsky made his braided tasseled jersey cap now hanging down in front of his face in an assorted array of colors.

It was 1985, one year later, and my partner, Michael, my son, Elan, and I had moved to Northampton. Calvin Coolidge bridge was under construction, and reaching UMass each day for classes was a potential traffic jam I didn't want to deal with; also, now 7 months pregnant with my second son. Subsequently, I applied for the 5 College Consortium exchange student program, to be closer to the radius where we now were living in Northampton and avoiding the Calvin Collage bridge altogether. I was accepted at Smith.

The first class I encountered there was a design class, and the assignment was to make a bridge. The bridge had to be substantial enough to last seven seconds with a quart of water over a span of 14 inches and made with toothpicks only. I did one. We, as classmates, each had a bridge that pretty much failed. Professor Lee Burns showed us a bridge that worked. It was made in two parts and the center would hold the quart via inertia. I held up my notebook and opened my sketch page of that design that I had drawn out but did not attempt to do.

The other students said they thought someone from UMass must have told me. I said, "no, no one did, I was just avoiding the bumper-to-bumper construction of the bridge, and that was why I was here at Smith."

I had 26 credits that semester, summing up my art thesis project. Along with the design class, I was taking Chinese Art History that was so interesting because it was linking my many years in 11th and 12th grade that I had studied the *I Ching*. The dynasties of art were so in tune with my studies of the *I Ching* that their Taoist ink paintings were seen in the brushwork. The space and mystery I fell in love with, triggering in me an instant euphoria just by looking at them. The space they rendered in patterns and markings. Before Chinese Zen Master of Art started to paint, they would do a pre-meditation ceremony.

Austin was in utero when I graduated from UMass, and I often thought he had a degree too through osmosis. I was the only one in class pregnant. I stood out, I mean Austin stood out. I had taken European Art History at Greenfield Community College, where I wrote up a paper on Northern Italy Madonna and Child. The professor said that my observations were astute and that she had been teaching the class for many years and had never seen these symbols for this Mother and Child oil painting interpretation.

In 1986, Austin was born. I then moved into the Quentin Quesnell home on North Farms Road. He was a professor at Smith College for many years. The wife invited me to her husband's lecture, and I informed her that I had gone to that college for a semester before graduating from UMass, but I let her know that with working at the jewelry story and nursing my children more than likely it would be something I could not attend. Persistence, again and again she kept reminding me right up to the day before, subsequently, I did acquiesce, and attend that lecture, sitting all the way in the back and I proceeded to fall asleep.

Before dozing off, I heard his introduction say Quentin Quesnell knows 9 languages. My landlord/genius started his talk and before falling asleep, I faintly recalled definitions I had heard going back to Sirius Bookstore, while in High School in Amherst. I heard the same word 'archetypal' in the same sentence as the founder of the college because I never knew that the college was supposed to be named Sophia Smith. Quentin went on to discuss the meaning behind Sophia and talked about her relationship between the alpha and omega circling through all life educating the group with this reference, then off into a dream I flew, recharging my batteries, sitting in the auditorium. I fell off into the abyss feeling this college was cooler than I ever knew, trying to stay awake, passing out.

The fine jewelry store I had been working in for a few years received the Advocate Jewelry Store of the Year Award. It had circa 500 B.C., Edwardian, Art Deco, and modern jewelry, including Patek Philippe watches. As manager there, with top sales I learned to let the stone connect with the customer. I looked at it as an exchange of energy. I gave the basic information then stepped aside, giving a pregnant space, letting the light of the gem do its magic. If that person didn't buy it right there then, they would be back.

The one time I went on vacation to Jamaica, the one country I have ever flown to, the one with the Brya tree, which I did not know then. I came back and was told that even though I was on a vacation to Jamaica, the sales went up. When returning they said that customers came in and bought what they had seen and connected to and were disgruntle wanting commissions that's why the whole idea wasn't conducive for comradery and subsequent poor personnel relations thus, perpetuated. I had to tell them about the magic space to give the sale near the end, let the stone sell itself, let the connection begin with you become the medium for the exchange of light.

I had a duchess-style sapphire my grandfather had given me with four tiny diamonds that sparkled just as brilliantly as large ones could. Like a flashlight in the night, accessible at any time, I could contemplate into it and feel a connection with the all the cosmos, right through its blue and white light rays. I gave a stone, a ring, pendent or bracelet informational stats to the customer, and then left a space for the communion between the person and the stone to take place. It was like clockwork. If I did this, giving this poignant opening, they would buy it.

On the other hand, if my boss took over and started to say anything more during this important silence, thinking he had to push the sale, push and object not for its beauty but for the money, of the two elements connecting, the soul with the stone, the sale would falter. I just knew whenever my boss was not there, I made one sale after the other. Somehow this message wasn't getting through to the owner, he didn't see the difference and I was not about to mention it to him. As soon as the interruption into the sacred silence between gemstone and recipient occurred, the sale stopped. Competition in commission I felt ruins the real exchange.

At this juncture, I had to find daycare. Only one had an opening for two children, the others had an opening for only one child, and this would mean taking my sons to two different centers, before and after work. It was in the St. John's Episcopal Church at Smith. Nonotuck Daycare. I went to the three-day orientation with Austin. Austin took off on the pathway at the inner commons and ran up the steps to Hillary Art Museum. He had on his Oshkosh rolled up jeans. I grabbed him just in time as a student opening the door was heading in. Wanting to be an artist, Austin?

I was making $1000 per month and day care was $800. My mom would send me 200 a month to help. In my eyes, it was all worth it. Pennies at the end. Getting to be with gemstones shining all around me was worth more than a paycheck could ever be. It was worth making the extra money even if the day care was taking 90 percent of my income. I loved the energy exchange through the power of the gems. Their light could absorb me. Heal me. Love into the world.

At Helen Hills Chapel Austin played piano in a duet with his teacher, Ms. Fearne. Bryce, Sr., came to take photos. Everyone had very complicated pieces. Austin had a simple song to play side by side with Paula. After the full solos with great crescendos and orchestration of flying fingers had finished theirs. Austin's song stood out. Each pause, each rest, pressing his finger down on the key, the timing, the cadences, rang through the silences, after the other awesome songs were done, and so busy, his simple duet could not help but stand out, with a gentle touch, you could feel his consciousness as palpable, not that the others were not bright, but their songs were a constant rhythm, without breaks, melodically staccato. The sound between the notes, in the silence, when it hits home, it's how the mind opens, it's when the heart merges, into its spaciousness, and all words vanish.

Maryanne Williamson of the Course in Miracles came to speak at John Greene Hall around 1993. I believe, as well, at this time, she had a few bestselling books out. At the end of the lecture Maryanne invited audience members, if they wanted, to come up to the podium and ask a question.

I had seen Christie from my high school years, the very first person I had done the Astrology Chart outside my family or my own. Chistie was in town a few times, and she had mentioned something medical to me but never any details. At the podium Christie told Marianne about her three weeks to live and right away Marianne had the audience make three circles around Christie and we all prayed along with Marianne. Christie went on and even twenty years later became a fund raiser for women's arts, a million dollars, truly in tune with her own chart I had read in 1973.

Shortly, thereafter, a Tibetan Death and Dying workshop was scheduled at thc First Churches in room 11. It was Elizabeth Kubler Ross' book which I had read many times earlier, learning the stages, for the first time, seeing behind the veil the profundity of a subject. After reading the book something stood out to me and that was the art of putting ghee or purified butter, with basil on the top of the head during the dying, or we could say, the birth of death, transition. The power behind pure butter from the Holy Cow, of which ceremonial sculptures are made in India.

Cows have multiple stomachs that process milk into its sacred medical uses, for one, it does not need refrigeration even after hundreds of years it is still good, and it can be placed on a cut, because it is astringent, anti-septic, plus this holy elixir called ghee goes right to the pineal gland, when we ingest it, also, it can handle high heat because other oils, longer molecules replace cells with radical toxins, only ghee and olive oil, have a shorter molecule allowing higher heat tolerance while cooking.

The most significant ghee applications however is in combination with it and basil, which has strong negative ions and high in bioflavonoids, a spiritual potent, deliverance at the point of transition, raises the highest possible consciousness level up, propelling one, closest to their destination in the next lifetime, ascension. I could understand why, after learning all this, why it's so useful to the loved one's soul existing at the highest point in the body, this application assists.

When the class in First Churches in room 11 talked about letting the deceased go, truly just remembering happy memories and letting go of anything else because the loved one here can hold back the one that has moved on. It triggered me to look at the 23 years with Eileen's voice.

This class provoked me to question this and why I have her voice, clear as day, just happens just surfacing at times I had never correlated if they synchronized with anything, in any concrete way, were instead just straight from heaven. That night I had a dream and woke up to a memory. The next day, I had the same memory in the dream. The third day, it played exactly again and I had to ask myself, "How come I am having dreams that are real memories?" I had to put the words into the silent movie.

And I then recalled hearing my mom say how Eileen had died of a head injury and this is exactly when I had buried my emotions. The doll breaking from the second-story window was holding me there in this moment, now a still life formed, with the guilt I felt, thinking I caused her death in some way with my harsh words. The truth came out, and my childhood flooded back through me. Each day in the shower or eating, buried segments of my life, the herstory of my memories reconnecting my life to the present. Boom, I gained back my emotional circuitry.

Out of nowhere, for 23 years, Eileen's giggle resurfaced, clear as day, for no apparent reason, and I never asked myself why, I never questioned it. It did probably happen upon a pattern, it probably happened each time in response to a need, or message coming through. But While in my heart, so torn, with my soul and an invisible grief, staying separated, in myself, between the two, wanting to say goodbye to her, and to thank her for always appreciating our friendship. I needed to somehow merge.

I didn't know that would be the last time seeing her, I needed to be able to say I was sorry for the doll was no big deal, just a material thing and not as important as her. She had always shared with her words to me, but I had never shared with her, my feelings. My mother snapped me out of it one day, pointing her finger into my face. "Now Brya, you are going to die if you do not eat." Die. The reality somehow sunk in. I started eating the next day after three months, and down to 70 pounds, it was a slow gain, but gain nevertheless.

I didn't know I was closer than ever to Eileen now, after her death, 24/7. She gave me the power to go deeper with this pain, and to go high like a kite to the sky on just a thin thread, just a whisper, a word, light, with my new mantra Ieeme and Eileen disappearing into each other, merged into a transcendence, in correlation to its occurrence. And a harmonious mantra, not like the other ones growing up, in a small city, a metropolis, with a mantra mother.

It does not matter if it is a huge rope or just a thin thread to heaven, a connection is complete, whole, there are no measurable scales, one thin thread is still a megaphone connection, if we do not judge.

I learned to be happily unhappy, accepting unacceptance in me as the foundation of compassionate self-love. A warm love, combining higher consciousness of universal love to our wounds, here, merged.

The eyes, the duality, the first petal of life, the first flower, the first seed, eternally expressed through duplication through propagation through truth, genesis, a self-organizing template of life, forever blossoming, echoing, recycling the word, the sound, the mantra of existence, creative power of love.

Seeing Bryce in the ICU after his surgery wasn't easy. There is a loud penetrating, echoing off the cold cement walls, beeping, like a seat belt warning signal. It was a four-hour supposedly simple vein reconstruction that turned into 14 hours and many transfusions. The nurse is standing in front of the meter watching the blood pressure down blasting with warning sounds blaring. Bryce is covered over with a large starch pressed white linen sheet with tubes and wires all around him so I can't even see him, he is hidden beneath, even his face, covered. I felt like I was in a car driving without my seatbelt. Beep, Beep, Beep. I said why is that going off and the nurse responded that it was a blood pressure drop. Just then his arm reached out with an open palm from under the covering, and gracefully, gently ever so softly, landed, cupping my face to my left cheek. His big soft warm palm comes out embracing my face. My thoughts, my eyes. I was transformed. I went there to support him, but instead, incapacitated Bryce, gave me something boundless.

Seeing Bryce a few days before was shocking, he was looking like an office paper collating project with more staples than I could, would or wanted to count, going up the interior of his leg. What happened to normal regular stitches, with string, I thought, now were metal. Staples have to have someone press into something, to clasp it closed. This much I knew, and could only imagine from experience, from executive administration work at the hospital PHO, at the church, at the president's office at Greenfield Community College, at the Whitmore Administration, Transfer Affairs office, and all the work studies stapler experiences, when you use a stapler, you must press down.

A stapler needs to close its clasp up against something. I did not want to question how this long row of metal in a leg could be administered, could be facilitated, could be applied, was devasting to see. I just wanted to know how they got those into him, did they have to press into his bones. However, this was not the issue.

He gave me some odd story about being in the army and drinking for the first time and getting drunk and sick and never wanting to ever drink again in his life. A story I had never heard and was wondering what the real meaning of this story pointed to, was not evident to me yet.

I came back two days later, and he was in pain. Ten days since surgery so I asked for tests. They said no, you must wait it is the weekend, and the doctors went home at 5. It was 6 pm on a Friday. The nurses furthered that only the maternity ward has an ultrasound, and he can't use it. I wanted him to be able to use the maternity ward and asked again for it. They then called the doctor on the phone and called me over to the station to speak with him directly. He also said that our father would have to wait until the morning. I hung up and told them I wanted to unplug my father and then how I should take him down to their emergency room and get him admitted downstairs. He had not eaten in over a week, yet he had gained weight, it was not making sense.

They called the doctor back and I was informed I could have a cat scan for him, now was available, at midnight. I gave him the drink while we looked into each other's eyes, his one blue and one green eyes. I saw the ocean in the blue one. I saw the beach, I saw me running through his eye, through the sand, toward the low tide ocean and how it kept going it reached out into infinity. There was no end. I saw his light. I whispered to him, "I love you", and he said it back and later many months after, it came to me, I realized he was deaf and heard my whisper.

Then an invisible source of energy came into the room, and it formed into a pillar of light from the floor of his room next to me and the bed, to the ceiling, was like a beam of light, and this beaming light, had a tireless eternal ceaseless feeling coming out of it, a grace, a divine emanation. I felt yes, he is getting healed he is going to be fine his angels are here. Just then a nurse came in to report to me that the cat scan cannot be used because someone in the ER must use it, now. I thought it was a drunk person, probably, and Bryce had the appointment first, brushing him aside.

I looked over at him, back into his eyes. I kissed his face. It dawned on me, then, I am in my selfish ego wanting him to go this way, my way toward me, toward what I call life, staying here. Instead, I felt a powerful natural loving flow pulling him toward his life, his path. Bryce's soul was heading its own way toward its own direction bringing me this peace, as if a mediator was with us, the Holy Ghost. This meant he was going to ascend, but instead I became engulfed in the living light that this transition was emanating with more love than I had ever experienced in my life, had ever to encountered, standing before me, beaming down like a crystal of the highest grace powerful enough to bring one to their knees, through heard consciousness, door or portal. I had to ask if this was a light for me too, not just transitional light, but a light that bids me the power to say goodbye, so easily now, a grace a love of all compassion that prevails on both sides, the Holy Ghost highest function pertains.

By morning, he was taken down, around 4 am to cat scan, finally, and the machine a brother said, was out of juice, without a blanket and naked, pushing him back into his room and closed the door on us. We ran down to the lounge to wait. We heard 'code blue STAT' over the wing intercom, and the reason was shockingly for our dad, and I could not fathom. The voices seemed separate, the noise aggravating. I just held onto that peace he had in his room, was now all before him, an opening, a window, from the heart. I held onto the doctor's hand as he escorted us down to the room. The door was still shut, a round energy like invisible ball came right through the middle of the door and I said, "Dad, I can see you," as it went down the hall so fast and out the window flying at top speeds. This ball never materialized only to me was a ball, shapeless edgeless but very real.

It went down the hall and out the window. And I said to myself, "Dad you do not have to follow stairways and roads anymore; you are free to fly." The reason I so love birds. That someone above me, in this life, has grown wings. There he went like a firefly, like an owl, like a comet, but inside I knew this was not a goodbye but a major hello, from the other side, just beginning in a whole new way.

I walked into his body lying there, looking so peaceful like Christ with his beard and bald head, so beautiful. The doctors kicked something under the bed and the wall had one of those plastic measuring cups hung on the wall filled with red liquid. His story of the over drinking, sunk in.

Matt had gone outside and said a wind came as he leaned up against the building and blew off his hat.

I got home somehow, without thinking, and was sitting at the back yard picnic table. A wind came and a leaf blew up to my spot. We used to hike at Quabbin, the place he felt he was the last person on earth, so expansive. The next day I awoke under my skylight not sure if I had had a nightmare or if it was true to life really happening and asked my partner. He said, "No, it's real, he has died."

Looking up, I could see the same leaf that had blown up onto the picnic table was now stuck to the rain drops on the window. I had broken the stem. Now the snapped stem, the same exact leaf was looking at me from above, from the skylight glass, just sitting there, as I lay there looking up at the reflection of myself, with the world outside, shadows overlapping and the world of the other side opening, with memories flooding in. I felt a shock being between two worlds colliding.

He had sold his house and traveled in his blue van with his Coleman stove, plaid blanket, pipe, and Nikon camera setting up tripods with timers to take self-portraits of himself in front of old abandoned adobes. Each time with a different hat, a French barrette, an English cap, a cowboy hat, a sailor's hat, a bandanna. With a long beard he did double exposures of buffalo grazing on his van, with him standing there, transparent.

He was a rare man in that he was truly what he seemed to be. No airs. Accepting everyone equally. And a man with little words and liked things to be a through z. He used to yell at me if I talked back, closing his eyes and pursing his lips, saying, "Young lady, do not get wise with me." I always thought, "I will always want to be wise." So, his words were punishment, restricting the very heart of my existence. At the same time a mile marker in my life pointing out what I would always thrive to be, putting a tack right in it.

I brought his ashes to the Quabbin, in a bowl on a windless day then while reaching the water's edge and just placing the bowl carefully down, a sudden burst of wind and the ashes flew up directly into my face, onto my cheek.

The ashes only hit my cheek not my eyes, nose, or mouth, and it was like a kiss, it was like his palm at the ICU reaching out and cupping my face in a warm love of fathering peace.

In the morning there were doves above his van, waiting for him. Twin doves on a telephone wire.

It was one week later, and I had read the *'Death and Dying'* by Elizabeth Kubler Ross a long time ago, but I remembered her giving a timeline to the souls tethering out after death, and the letting go, stages were called the states of Bardo. I walked into his room to get any feel for this and was suddenly given exactly where he was and went walking with him through it, and yes it was a real process, just like the book I did assist in walking him through one of the levels.

On the cover of the sports page of the Daily Hampshire Gazette is Elan, up in the air his hat on backward, hitting his powerful backhand to the baseline for the winning point in a 3-hour 100-temperature heatwave match for the final Western Mass Title, at the Smith tennis courts athletic field. It was the Carrington Tennis school training done near Hampshire College, years before. But it was reminiscence of the birth of Elan under the sycamore tree where I had him up in the air and his jersey cap falling sideways.

A mirror from 13 years prior, reflecting similar images left engrained in nature all around us, memories left in the air, the water, keeping tabs, records, alpha data of conscious the conscious life within us, it was synchronicity. It was a thread, the language of light, the alpha and omega of the meaning of Sophia. The two images reflecting each other, almost exact and the open invitation of Sophia Smith to let student teams compete on their campus was paramount to their graduations, piano concerts, skating on the pond each winter, my 5 College classes, my volunteering in the Lyman Botanical and the Course in Miracles lecture that I witnessed Christie's miracle, the Art class with Professor Rhea, and Lee Burns, and my landlord, Quentin Quesnell's, invitation to a lecture that pointed out so many facts linked to Sophia and myself, all these years, she following me, I or me her, all at Paradise. The Paradise of the Campus set out to be a spiritual school named Sophia Smith but was changed to just Smith, and the spiritual mission changed.

In the book, *The Look of Paradise*, by Jacqueline Van Vorhis, under education, page 57, it states, "Sophia Smith left the bulk of her estate to found a college for women in the belief that by the higher and more thorough Christian education of women, what are called their 'wrongs' will be redressed, their wages adjusted, their weight and influence in reforming the evils of society will be greatly increased, as teachers, as writers, as mothers, as members of society, their power for the good will be incalculably enlarged."

Growing up Christian Scientist with my great-grandmother, Cassie, Aunt Golda and her sister, Thelma, and my mother, I learned the basic statements. After reading the Bhagavad Gita translation at the same time as reading Science and Health by Mary Baker Eddy, it became evident to me that the two books were very similar in spiritual perspective. Both believe in the God Source as right now, living in us. Catholicism and most Christian religions believe it is only at the point of death, when we die, that the soul is saved, yet Christ never died, he lived.

They both talk about the perfect reflection of God, is alive in us, now. While most catholic and other denominations of Christianity believe in waiting until death.

I heard that Sophia was also supposed to be the name of Smith College. Sophia, the founder's first name, was dropped. I saw it in a Paradise history of Northampton book. So, I gravitated over to the Neilson Library and got out the booklet of the lecture I had attended right after Austin's birth passing the Smith College Seal on my way.

I read that Sophia Smith died on June 12 and I am born on June 12, I read that in fact the school was to be spiritual or a Christian curriculum. I am all about faith. I witnessed a miracle there by a Marianne. I read further that Sophia's brother that helped to fund the college was named Austin and I named my son Austin. Reading the pamphlet by Quentin Quesnel, from the lecture I had attended, it furthered that Sophia's housekeeper was catholic and she left a birthday card for Sophia that lived in Hatfield with the Lady of Guadalupe on it on the table.

The Seal of Smith college has the same similar rendering as this image, this archetype. The 12 stars above her head left out. Those are the 12 constellations, showing, as above so below, of in the Bible it relates to that are in other rendering of This Spanish Madonna pregnant. I attend there because of being pregnant and not wanting to cross the Calvin Coolidge under construction twice a day. Most Madonna and Child are depicted with Christ born already and on the lap of Mary, however in the Lady of Guadeloupe, she is expecting, as too, attending Sophia Paradises, I was, as well participating there in the same way, insemination similarities, or call this a synchronicity of fated myth, writing my pages for me, as I write.

I had moved to Amherst in 1971, and Smith started in 1871, one hundred years, hence. I saw the synchronicities and felt if she was following me or me her and how I had never met her, but she was in my life in vicarious ways which I could see even in the Miracle of Christie by Mary(Anne) unfolded and how Sophia wanted her college to be of Christian or Spiritual academia curriculum but when Sophia Smith died, it all changed. Sophia Smith passed before it opened and her first name so significant and so powerful has the PHI built right in it. The Tree of Life sequence, of which the name meaning wisdom has the phi or 5 representing the pattern of life, the Golden Ratio of the Vitruvian Man by Leonardo DaVinci, was dropped and the school to be spiritual was neglected and ignored. And to think, Sophia Smith College also had a president named Carol T. Christ. I think someone needs to look at what Sophia from the other side is saying through me, through my life, this coherent continuum, a spiritual paradise. And now you can access their paradise campus, through TreeSpeak audio and photos.

Just like states of mind which are always are open, because I go there without a teacher, I am so exited within to go on adventures while standing still, reaching out, reaching in, the same movement, all within me, then afterwards, I find the book that pertains to that very experience on a bookstore shelve. I find each step I took to the Thomas Father Keatings book, '*Open Mind Open Heart*' and '*The Secret of the Golden Flower*,' and others.

Light finds light. I went on my own, that inner adventure
before reading it and it came to me after as confirmation.

Weeping Beech Tree

When the branches sweep your face and the leaves comb your hair, you have entered the sanctuary of the Pendula, weeping beech tree at Sophia Smith.

Every inch of Pendula's smooth thin bark around her trunk, and up to some of the branches have been carved, etched, scripted with monograms, initials, and autographs. Some are in block, some in cursive, some are drawings of a heart. She remains alive, and well, on the campus of Sophia, inscribed by scholars, with the ALPHA-bet.

The Pendula tree grows deep down, rises high up, and cascades down with thin tentacle type sweeping thin branches like that of the willow. You can't miss her, but you can. Her green sweeping thin branches reach all the way down to the grass. Pendula's trunk cannot be seen, it's a sanctuary, it's a shelter, hidden, camouflaged. When you do see her, you think you are looking at Cousin It from the Addams family. Her plume reaching down all the way with her branches re-rooting, sucking up water around the exterior, because her thick overlapping dangling dreadlocks, so thick a coat she wears, is acting like a rain repellant, keeping out wind as well. She knows and will share her knowledge with you. Grounded in Mother Earth and extending up into Father Heaven if you let her, she will open. You will hear her answer in stereo surround sound, from the birds, squirrels, rabbits around you.

This one thing I remember from the tarot teacher at Arcadia Wildlife Sanctuary in Easthampton workshop had designed her own Tarot cards with equality in mind. Kings and queens were replaced with a full spectrum of social diversity, with some voluptuously endowed, the whole real-life array, from its ancient beginnings. This artist, tarot card teacher, let us know that if one is to ask a tree something, or commune with the tree, one needs to ask it permission before going closer.

It's like the Tree of Life, their calls at first light weaving out into space, the garden, because we are free from their words, the sounds do the magic, the magic of the PHI, the dendritic pattern, blueprint of life, the fingerprint of God, the tree, the lightning the electric static, bursts into light, clearing the ozone, bringing in a current, a battery, recharging life, the soul. Sound and vision merged.

In the beginning was dark. She was here first. Her all potential, all-pervasive, deep dark essence, her peacefully powerful being, her womb, her freedom of space, no boundaries, no race, just is. Nameless, the dark mother came first. The word sparked vision. Light is not just the sun. Light is a thought wave, and it with the dark, creates emotion, movement, growth. Blossoms from the soil always start in the dark. Unless you see the two, see the shadow is restful light. The dark is light too. It is a being. Pure black is all thoughts all at once, all inventions, all concepts all thinking, the cave of the womb, the heart and love. The resting places where love creates a pull a gravity. Dancing together.

The electrical and the magnetic. The Father/Mother and the Holy Spirit, the Joy, the New, the Blossom, the Birth is the Inner Child, the Eternal Youth. YOU. Compassion, joy, all emotion, is the colorful rainbow, the only real thoughts to think unless one is building a house or solving a problem, real freedom, real space, real love. The dark holds all colors blended, and the light, is the absence. In heaven, in joy, light is all colors and dark are absence. In the beginning was the word, which echoed back from the being, the dark being of pure potential. It created the womb, the circle the loop the flower the first petal the eyes, the eternal recycles, back and forth, the echo the word, the point of existence to be in form, to integrate universal love.

I had shuffled the oracle earth card the day before and received the Eagle card. Upon arrival, far above, hardly visible was an eagle making circles. Confirming with us a higher love creates synchronicity. Pure vision is pure energy.

Dreams from heaven appear on earth. They know what they are doing, dancing in the air with arches. Circles, Loops. Our visions guide us on into what we think is movement. Movement is the landscape, the pallet of life. Movement is not going anywhere, it is LOVE. Life seeing itself. A stream flowing is going nowhere, nothing is moving. It's all water. It is standing still, but we see currents. This is LIFE. The flowing ocean of love, in our hearts hears the voices, our ancestors, their stories, their voices, their songs.

Stepping inside you are now surrounded by her long-extended wiry interlacing branches. The strands landing out from Pendula gnarled 50-foot-high and three-foot thickened trunk like a water fountain, delicately flowing down taking root blocking the sun but still the sun gets in, in crescent opening, landing in circles on and around the trunk of the tree, however, although.

Almost like the way a weed will grow through cement, light makes its way in, it's all-pervasive pattern of photosynthesis, always a green light for light to find light, a magnet through the pattern set in stone, the PHI of Sophia, in the template of life. The living art of the unfolding spiral. The fabric. So, PHI is life curving in the bigger picture, and on the smallest scale, turning. This is the Pendula at Sophia Smith, her paradise, her 'So PHI a' of wisdom and knowledge.

The sun blinds us to our own light, but in the dark, we find it.

Prior to working at the health resort in the Berkshires, I had been in secretarial and accounting, hospital and forensic engineers managing, doing quarterly taxes. Now I am living on the mountain, dead-end, dirt road, 900 feet up above sea level in a house Mayril had started to build but never finished, just sitting there empty for twenty years. I asked her if I could move in there. The first order of business was to get the bats out. Otherwise, I found a job looking in a local bulletin, Many Hands. It was asking for a Psychic. It would be an interview process in the spotlight when this I thought was a very calm smooth no judgment meditative state of mind, pre-requisite and would I be able to merge the two, conundrum. Can I be psychic in a pinch, under the wire? Is this a conflict of mind needing a certain outcome where the soul, needs none, will I be able to trust in the flow.

After three interviews, I made it in. I was afforded my lifelong studies, applications in astrology; the As Above so Below, handwriting analysis, palmistry, and numerology, using numbers as guides to uncover trends and messengers, doing lectures, business parties, demonstrations.

I had just been an office manager for a forensic group, chemical and structural engineering firm that had a burn victim case come in. I guessed the fire started from static. The Yale Graduate said it was from hot pipes. It was later confirmed that the cause was static. I knew so well having long hair and in the winter it stands up on end near to water even more so and the photo of the client had long hair.

I don't think taking a lot of science would have gotten me anywhere, different. I don't think math would give me the formulas that I know. In fact, even physics has it wrong and even the whole universe has the science wrong. It's just electricity. That's it. The yin yang, interchanging.

Carnations

She sat down and asked if I could contact her husband that died, and she has never gotten any messages from. "It's been two years," she added, and no signs. I instantly received a vision but felt hesitant in saying it. Most people want roses or tulips. So, I said it bravely without listening to my logical mind, "He wants to give you carnations."

She started crying and laughing all at once. He used to say he was going to go get me some flowers, and I would say back to him as he went out the door, just don't bring me back carnations. He had a sense of humor, so she knew it was him, with her, again, and still she was shocked to remember him so closely, feeling freed.

Then a woman came in and sat down and said her sister had died and can I reach her. Instantly, my hand went up into the air, something had me open my palm and a ball fell into my hand. Invisible but real. I said I see a ball, its small, it fits into my palm. She said, "Oh my god, that was what she last said to me, her final words were to keep playing golf without her. She and I went all the time together."

A woman had lost her son seven years earlier. She just could not get over it. I asked about a possible younger son. She said, yes, she has one and that he is always drawing flowers. I said that is from the other son to you. She talked more about the drawings. We investigated in a mirror. The following year, her sister came to the Berkshire health retreat and said how much I had helped her sister and how much her sister's whole life had changed, finally letting go of the trauma of her son's death. Dying into the self, rebirthing, and feeling life again.

Once, a client came back and stopped me in the hallway, saying, "I don't know if you remember me, or our session you did for me last year. I did exactly what you saw in my chart to become a yoga teacher. I started up as a yoga teacher and my whole life has changed and everything you said came true and is so great."

One woman, a retired professional in a large company, came in and I did her chart. In her wheel at the apex is Chiron the asteroid for childhood wound, the same wound is also our greatest gift, archetype, meaning it was in the position of profession of the tenth house, career. I said, "You have a job that is unique, it is about broken people, wounded, hurt."

She responded with, "Well, I am retired now, but I worked for a company as an investigator finding criminals."

Then the 8th house—for sexuality, rebirth, intense, power—I saw in another guest's chart. It was filled with certain planets that directly pertained to intensity. Both the house and the planets found at her birth in that house gave a strong indication that her job was the ruler of sexuality, power, birth and death, and it was ruled to other people's assets, resources. Clearly, I said to her, "You are a lawyer and do sexual abuse cases."

She said, "How do you know that? I am one of four lawyers in Canada, and I do companies that have sexual allegations." She gave me a distrusting look and said, "I don't believe this, you must have looked me up." Little did she know, I had no time or need, it was in the chart, the 12 constellations are our 12 strands of DNA, each a sound wave that creates a form, a template to our 12 holes in the body and 12 structures of the body.

Once, a young man came in. I opened his chart. He wanted to know specifically about his career. He want me to let him know what he would be best at achieving. I opened it and told him. His mouth dropped and he went over to his nap sack, opened it, and showed me the exact college books he had just bought for the classes he was going to take overseas. It was a confirmation. We already know our charts, but it sets the course on track. We come into this world, I believe setting a plan, down of what to learn, experience, and share, then we go.

Charts are confirmation that the universe already knows what you are doing, we are like in a car, on remote control.

Astrology charts are the six-pointed star of David. The six points have six spaces. The double trinity. Pointing to heaven and earth. We have instant knowing, in our genes. Our bodies cells remember millions of years back or would not be here. We respond to life in this way, by asking and waiting for the universe to respond we can keep to our individual strategies, moving forward. It is easier than we think. Trust the universe, trust the design, the Genesis of Life, the template that forms in the womb, woman, room. The 13th full moon at the center of the 12 Holy Men or 12 Disciples or 12 decuples. The 12 Holy Men have 12 holes in their body but Mary, a woman, we have 13, one extra. Of which the 12 strands to our DNA have are the 12 possible sound waves, or notes that make 8 possible scales of which there is 8 notes each making the 64 codons. Which is also the six lines that are six spaces and make up the Star of David. The religion, stars and science of the 5 platonic solids merge into the designing of the heart mechanism to fold down, to collapse without getting injured, from and into a cohesive design, of Metatron's cube with the beginning of the Bible stating God is a tetragrammaton.

If you play the hertz sound of the solfeggio sound waves to a plate with rice or sand, it will vibrate into the outline of the star of David. Form is from sound. The twelve constellations, and 9 planets, are lined up with our human energy chakras, spinning frequencies that create from this sound this word the human anatomy template in the deep dark protective womb of pure love, unfolding, in the spiral from, first heartbeat to amphibian to reptile to human stages and the placenta has the Tree of Life pattern. Showing how the sound of the DNA and RNA sine wave is both the first template and the light of now, mixed, weaving together this human, form, interconnected to all life forms throughout the planetary galaxy. Dense form but can travel with light ray vibrations to ascension and pure love or bliss, very easily, our innate, intrinsic soul blossoms, grows, while standing still.

The last reading, I did was with a mom who had lost a son to an overdose. He started to tell her, through me, how she is acting like she is addicted to his death now. I got her to laugh, we found all the contributing factors holding her back from directly communicating with him, and the meaning around having a second child with similar traits, still living in the house with her. Her son started to give me tips to tell her about his sister's predicament. The mom felt so relieved to be talking to him, directly, as he knew so much about her state of mind. It all makes sense somehow on a symbolic psychological level what things we are going through, and the inner need of the self is a mirror. Unclear boundaries in herself, her daughter mirrored.

I noticed when an aspect in the heavens is happening, like three planets forming a grand trine, I would have guests that had the same aspect come in, in clusters. All at once that week. The interesting thing about that was, they made the appointment weeks, sometimes months before, converging into synchronicity. The natal chart, the symbols on the paper seemed to come alive when the guest would come in. Sometimes I would be given their birth data ahead, and opening the chart would say some things to me, evident information, but when they would walk in and I would be seeing into the chart, it was like it would open into a dimensional portal.

Sometimes, as I was reading a chart to a guest, just before getting to the next archetypal message, the comments that the guest would start to say or tell me would be directly related to the next symbols I would be going to talk about. I would say you are reading your own chart, and you have never had it done before. The symbols would almost bounce around giving me clues of where to go next.

Just think we are born alone, die alone and never meet anyone. It's all the energy we attract that is happening. We have good intentions, we want the best, but life is a mirror.

One guest was now a widow and wanted to make sure that a partner she was starting to date was not just after her money. The tarot cards, with the natal and progressed transits, were saying she had met something that was exactly her fears. We talked about fears and we did some affirmations, blessing her to clear and open.

Sound waves of binaural hertz healing solfeggio help unite thoughts and heart or align heart with mind. Singing bowls and chimes clear the atoms in the water in the body that have images stored on a cellular level. A memory from the womb, from the heart of pure sound in the mother's womb. Of pure life. Of pure energy. Charged seedlings into starlings into young stars. The Gregorian chants were tuned into these special notes that raise the vibration of the heart. The chords were lost. Listening to them increases the pineal gland secretion of the bliss hormone. Using head bands with these tones, one hertz different than the other hertz named binaural, will bring states of alpha without addiction and be effective no matter how much you listen to it. Each ray of sound going into the gland hits in an orbital location in the glands, creating a vibration. It can be used in progressive healing practices for depression. Creating alpha waves.

In January of 2017, Mayril suddenly dies. Within weeks of finding out, I go shopping and pick out boots, try them on in the store, then again at home. I see they are not my style, a suede, wrinkled up at the ankle, looking frumpy to me, plus to try them on twice, at the store and again getting home, was not like me either. This was my mom trying to talk to me. I didn't like how she would make me try things on many times. At the Muppet Shop then getting home again.

I grew up and made sure not to go through this myself. Just buy something that looks nice, looks the right size and bring it home, then if I need to wear it, try it on then. That was it, that was simple. "Brya, it's Mayril, I am here," was what all this was saying to me. It was two weeks after her death and was very clear. This was how she got in, the very place I disliked, into my heart again.

From there, I started to design clothes and each thing that I did, so unique, so different, I could feel her smiling, hear her laugh, feel her presence so easily. One design is a something I have never seen yet, anywhere on anyone.

Mayril found this way into me, into my brokenness, the thing I she loved, I disliked about her, doing to me, now was the most beautiful thing. This is where I found the heart can heal love both ways, and more we can heal into the past or into the future in this transcendence of dimensions. Whether we do it for the one we dislike, the one that gives us grief, gives us headaches, or the one that we love, it is the same difference, love has no sides, no opposites. We think in this world that hate is the opposite of love. When love is the essence of life itself, the core element. The actual chemistry, that we feel as mothers, with a child growing in the womb. This string, this thread of light, of memory, is in all things always, wanting to be acknowledged, is the source of our growth. The meaning of life, the progress of the soul. Life's only true message, only true purpose, expanding love.

Taking my stuff finally out of storage, after years of being in the attic at her home, I read the directions which stated to sweep the room clean when leaving. It was clean. There was nothing to sweep. One photo with scalloped edges was turned over on the floor. I walked over to it and picked it up. It was a black and white photo of my mom.

How did that get out of my photo box, I thought and why didn't any other photos fall out with it? I knew it was my mom at around 8 years old. Then looking closer at the photo, I could see she was holding a doll. The doll with the broken head that everyone had told her to throw out, but told me how she would not.

Mayril wrapped the doll up in a blanket and strolled it around. It reminded me of my first death of this lifetime, and how it was similar. My mom and I both had a significant experience with a doll. I felt DNA is one thing, but perhaps it goes even deeper. Perhaps the very visions we hold of things, like when looking into a pond, but our bodies made of 78 percent water, hold memories we generate from our hearts, of things we saw that left a mark on our hearts, are stored and passed through our DNA. It seemed so.

It hit me that another message was included there, that she was also saying what she taught me from 60 years ago, always put yourself in other people's shoes, looking down at her, now up in heaven. Looking down at how she used to dress me, now liking it from high up in heaven, a message so clear. This was a significant turning point, how all light turns, all things come back around like Karma, like memories, thoughts. And now the scope of love that still walks on, this memory, in the light, reborn.

Walking in other people's shoes, with the doll, the doll she also had, the best friend of mine that dropped a doll down into the grass, same strongly similar images recorded in our life.

At one of the elder homes I worked at doing activities was sweet Gertrude H. She was 105. A tiny lady at that listened to classical music on an old victrola, and blind. I saw her in her room, over the turntable, playing another album of classical music walking by each day. Music is a thread of light, of love.

Gertrude and I would walk down the long hallway together looking at each painting on the wall and I would tell her what the theme of the painting was, what style, what colors were prevalent. Describing for her all the textures and scenes of the whole row of hanging paintings right to the last one, of 30 at the end of the hall. It was a nice exchange, I got to use my art history expertise and she got to remember what it is to see.

When I went to work the next few days, I saw she had decided to stop her medications and I went in and tried to give her a sip of water. The next day when I came in, I was told how she passed away that morning. As I was walking down the hall, so sad, I saw that every single painting was an inch tilted to one side. I smiled inside. It was Gertrude that made sure to say thank you and goodbye all in one hallway to me.

My father was easy, he gave me messages through leaves. If I had to reach him or had something going on, a leaf would appear on my windshield.

As I stepped out onto the storage lot, I could see one leaf spiraling down. It was summer and no other leaves were anywhere to be seen on the asphalt nor in the woods behind it. I had the photo of my mom in one hand, holding a doll, and my arm reached up. I saw the leaf floating side to side, to step where it was going, but I had to stop to be Still, I did not try to move or judge or sway. I stood with my palm open and it lands exactly where I was standing only taking two steps to reach it, as I shouted HI DAD, dad is here now too.

I had him in the other hand. The leaf. He was saying, "Brya, I will not leaf/leave you. You are in the palm of my hand."

I was the one that left, that divorced from my partner I was the one that had one foot out the door for many years in my marriage, yet two years later I find myself still emotionally attached and call him about something. I had to do something about this. Asking myself where is the thread that binds us and hoped prayer would clear it away. Clear me up. Open my vessel once again entirely. I took the pain with my hands on my heart and lied down on the couch to have a serious talk with myself and out came this dark cloud, lifting from my body like a shadow, then I heard a pop just like popping a balloon, I thought it would hurt more open to the pain but the reverse was true, the universe absorbs pain when you love it away, which was already the same amount of pain inside holding keeping still, so why would feeling it fully make it any bigger, it is the opposite, the more we feel not with the mind, against the mind but truly from the heart, trusting that emotions have a high intelligence then the more one keeps clearing their field keeps balancing their energy, staying alive and well.

Most people, hold it in too long then can't tolerate emotions from someone else letting theirs be discussed. Or even thinking at that point that the other person is crazy, but it is the non-responsiveness, the non-emotions not duplicating the other ones feelings that stop the whole process from flowing from working from doing its magic. By holding onto, this was condensing it smaller into a rock, a block, essentially preventing the flow of love. We think if we feel something it will get bigger, but this is the result when we do not feel, or express out, openly.

Life doesn't afford suitable avenues for our minds and emotions to be expressed, for a balance, our culture is pseudo intellectual, our hearts have to rule the show. We are top heavy, in our minds, lost, ungrounded in the actual peace the earth gives us through our feet. Just look at the animals, sleeping on the ground. They store chi force life energy, no words needed.

I was empowered not to feel less pushed down or deny but to feel more, in fact it opens the heart again and it lets us know that whatever you have been through, you are already feeling it, it is always within you. Only the gate of the heart can transform pain. Feel it for its message, go to the heart for the initial sign of grief, then bring it higher, using love, transformed.

The PowerPoint I presented had one small video clip and the first part I didn't need to show but did not know how to edit it out. I was just going to fast-forward it. However, when that part came, the computer shut down and the screen went dark. I managed to get the clip back up, and when it came back on, all on its own, it was back to where I was going to start it back up. The computer did it for me exactly to a T. Who says that the mysterious is not factual and exacting? Looking at the results, mystery is Scientific.

Color and consciousness are around us a reflection of our state of being from our associations to them. Black is absorbing, cleansing, pure power, relaxing, free. But when we hold onto negativity, we must see it bravely, this shadow side, the subconscious patterns of our lives, not hide from the dark, but use it, relax into with our consciousness, our awareness without reaction. But if it is too painful to sit with, although it's there in full effect anyway, brewing and getting smaller and smaller, denser and denser. It may take a few times to surrender and let it move, let it breathe, give it space, acceptance and like a mother, like in the womb, just be, awareness and free, the way we are made, our original self, light.

It finds you have no use for it, you do not need it; it does not need you. Poof, it disappears without a trace. No thoughts, no strings, gone. You cleared it. Honesty, hands on your heart. No memory of why an attachment was there; one is brought back to the eternity of life, that pure force that erases our thinking that forms into hardened neurosis and frees up our energy to be an open vessel.

'Ye shall do greater works as he has done, and live in the wonder of a small child, ask and Ye shall receive, be pure at heart, and Ye shall enter the kingdom of heaven.'
Matthew 18:2-4 John 14:12 Matthew 7:7

Works when we open to the mystery, honor the mystery, asking heaven. An example of this is, why am I so healthy? Instead of an egoic statement that also provokes the brain to do the opposite, think the reverse. If we say, I am rich, we are also saying, I am poor. Invoking both sides of the brain, both halves simultaneously. Instead, 'why' opens the life chi door, the mechanism to flow through energy from the brain thus, opens the whole body functions for more Chi, more love, more joy. Instead, instilling freedom, by saying, 'Why is my life so abundant?' or 'Why am I so healthy? 'Then leave it up to the universe to answer. We have asked the question, we have opened our minds, with our hearts allowing for the space to be filled with what we already are saying we have. Make it true by envisioning it ahead, the universe response to fill. Life is a two way street and questions spark the flames. Not to be answered in words but to start the wave throughout our body, of joy.

We die right now right here this is it this is the moment we are at when we face what we named, or think is death is no different than the same place we birth into, here, hear in the sounds, the word of genesis, template to LIFE at all times right up to our last breath we do not ever feel a death, death never comes but to the ones down here looking at it as a loss of something, are truly the ones that have closed down, and die, to let go, to open up, to learn to reach the higher love field our loved ones have gone to, they await our arrival not in physical form but in our embracing a greater love and joy with them.

Embrace that we have needs but not the need itself, is life, the grand hug, from both sides, the mystery and life, together a constant thread of love, sustaining the soul. Expanding into universal awareness of it all. The whole scheme of things, along with the mundane, go together. For me mindfulness is a recipe for numbness. Heartfulness is the path of our humanity. Like bees of a hive all buzzing around, they are sustained as a group, through their sound. Sound comes from the heart. Not in negative words. If you hear them from someone it is that they are hurting, a calling, also to higher love.

My father's leaf, the one that danced to a sudden wind and landed atop the picnic table, right where a plate would be, smack dab right in front of my face. When my brother died suddenly, and sitting outside his home, there in the street came a dust storm, a wind tipping over someone's item in the yard, then moving in front of my car, there was both my dad, Bryce and brother, Matthew in this dance together, twirling up towards heaven, an ascending duet, was gathered and was saying, "Look, dad has Matt and Matt has dad and they are very happy."

I heard the music from the forest trees, wrapping around me. I walked over to the brook to see where it was coming from, and realized the music from nature, the bubbles, going over stones and rocks, through tunnels and out, under trees was coming from the whole length of the brook.

We are all unique, but we are all the same. All of life has communion, through communication and connection with this same place, the heart, compassion, eternal love. It's this fabric, this cloth, this skin we are in. Flowing vessel of love of energy, we become the frame, or we are the flow. All is the same at differing speeds or vibration, as in the Star of David spins two trinities, one forward and one backward, and the soul at the center of its two pyramids, the great 51.5 or translates into PHI from So Phi A the 5-pointed star, the ARC degree, which is the pattern Venus makes travelling through space, and how Arch Angels arrive.

As much as our daily routines keep allowing us to remain conscious and whole, the same patterns end up boxing us in and becoming stuck and unconscious. I have found one needs to break out of the mold at times, to get back to that place of sovereign solidarity. That place where the flow is not material, but spiritual, the thoughts are not endless but eternal. Our strengths become our weakness, as we turn back to humbleness, back to the honoring of this great mystery we are all in, revived into real strength, the strength of purity, of innocence.

Like the first petals to a flower, from the circle of wholeness of God, the Sun, twists into an 8. Life giving, regenerating all seeing eyes, 8. The first echo of his word we are perfect as he is perfect in heaven, we see, we take flight, a seed, flew like wings, each side of the 8, feathers from this vibration, gliding higher and higher on the ethers, from this heart-centered wave, where we exist. For what is the sound of one hand clapping—it is the SIGHT.

This mantra created a current like wheel spinning from the left side of my body around down to the right. The emotions of my body would be controlled with this soundwave, this word, in a holistic manner passing over my mind thoughts brain area to control the two functions then back around. My energy was at one on a physical level, spiritual and mental levels, connected in a continuous stream and the water in my body mixing its emotions with the air, the thoughts were creating my particles in my body to levitate. This energy was so unifying that I could go without breath for I needed nothing. My fuel was the very fuel of goodwill to all mankind.

This three-month constant mantra I did while doing Hatha Yoga, which is movements with breath. The chi is stimulated in the body and in the air all around oneself it's a battery enhancer to the maximal attunement. *'Oh, violet flame, let the light guide me for beloved I am.'* These words flew me into a deep realm, all-pervasive light that was very purifying. A source that was coming from me and it was endless energy that suspended my soul into tranquility.

The source a blue peal, suspended before my third eye, had no spot or placement but surrounded my whole being with it. It created a indigo, purple, blue, violet 3-

dimensional ball that could hover in front of my eyes, connected to me in some electrical gravitation field. I felt I could see all the way around it, but it was only in front of me, about six inches away from my head, and it had a tranquility coming out of it and the energy is the real message; the suspended sphere seemed illusionary for a cause, or just a projection from another place refueling me.

A visitation from an angel through our crystalline patterns, the center pedal or hub of many rays touching on all of them at once, like a button that rules the heavens, was before me in an eye like manifestation, but just pure round color of emanating huge serenity. In Hinduism, it is called the Blue Pearl Attainment.

The Cones

I wanted to give back to geriatric nurses for giving so much. To take care of the caregiver through offering back massages, bringing my chair massage to nurses in the five elder homes, free on Sundays, with hopes as well to be asked to come back each month for them because their work went smoother, the elder patients were happier, a win, win situation. I gave a ten-minute chair massage. It's the principle that if the patient is to be put first, one must maintain the help as well. The two go hand in hand.

I learned this in bodywork training at Kripalu that my very stance and posture during a massage transfers better energy to the clientele if I too am comfortable and not holding or straining any body movements in my motions. So, I did around 50 nurses. I happened to also do the dermatologist office staff, manager and doctor at one facility where something powerful happened to myself and the manager.

The manager had told me she would not be getting one because she is sensitive and had had a bad experience with a masseuse that was too rash with her. She then decided to have one and I remember the light was coming in through a beam to the chair. I lifted my hands up to the light and said the lord's prayer softly. She came into the room and sat in the chair. I remember starting very slowly and the grace of my movement in the air came back with my hands making an archlike pattern from her neck and head back to my body. I rocked the air current with an infused intention.

Suddenly, something came from the palm of both my hands out and into her head. She was startled as I was. I pulled back and she said, "What was that?" I said. "Margaret, you felt that too?"

She said, "Yes."

I said, "Do you think we can try it again and see what it is because I do not know either and it is amazing whatever it is." She said okay, and again, in a soft intentional graceful way creating a current, I touched her head with a conscious light and bang there it was again. My hands started projecting a conelike pattern directly out of the palm of my hands in unison. It had a metal material, it was high techno, one cone then the next just like the shutter to a camera but a laser beam of some kind was coming out of me. This manager had me stop. I stopped. Leaving me incredibly surprised and baffled that spiritual light could create such a materialistic form.

The Pool Filter Chanting

We stopped after an hour of chanting '*Om Namah Shiva.*' We were at my house at 99 East Street situated between the foot of Mt Tom and the Oxbow of the Connecticut river. I said, "Do you hear that?"

My brother, Ben said, "No, what?"

I said, "I am still hearing the chant we did; it is lingering in the air."

I got up and looked out the window to see where it was coming from. I saw people at the neighbor's yard about fifty feet away sitting around their built-in pool. I listened more and asked how this can be, to myself. It was not stopping, it seemed to be coming from something over there. I had to surmise that it was coming from the filter.

Somehow the words were in the water, then going through the filter and it was likened to what they call Piezo Electric, or perhaps, how the pyramids generated a sound wave from the current of the water, the angle of the pyramid that has a special quality to keep plants alive without water and razors sharp like new, regenerative qualities the Egyptians knew all about in their silk wrappings.

Every morning and in each class at my month at Kripalu for bodywork training, we would start with an '*Om.*' Not before too long, about one week, I started to walk past a hallway that I could hear this 'Om' coming from the air. I asked someone what was down that hallway. They said that was the boiler room.

Years later, a three-day intensive on Thai yoga massage, I heard this again when I went to the end of the hallway. It was gurgling and not the same chant vibration, only regular machine on and off type sounds. I left and three days later, I heard that the boiler stopped working and the place had to shut down for a few days. It's all new now.

Now and Zen

When death happens, we never experience it. Death is not there, only life. There is no feeling to death, no pain or suffering. Death does not happen later, tomorrow, next year. When death or transition happens its right now, right here. It is the same exact moment as this one. This is where we die.

Right now, here. It's not going to happen. It never does. But when that transition occurs, that transformation, it's where we are right now, there is no difference. It's all the same place, the same time, the same moment. This is it. Be a present, it's the best gift to give. Open, enjoy, it's the ability we have and have always had. Freedom, the soul is not in a box to begin with, it is not contained. The soul flies. The soul dreams, the soul has wings, imagination, timelessness, spirit is creative and eternal, no boundaries. This is a story of the spirit.

No matter how deep we go, millions of miles into the tiniest neutrino, using stronger and stronger eyes, we just come out at the other end of eternity because we are looking, we are studying ourselves. We are the question and answer all in one. The question is just our mind, but the soul, the heart knows exactly what everything is, is love, is emotion. Every thought, every tear, every moment is love.

This numeric existence of creation is feminine. The divine feminine, in each of us, is true. The universe is electrical, it is negative and positive. The emotions or body is magnetic and the sun, the is the vision, the idea. From the word came from, from out of the dark, womb the pretexting mother of all creation came the first star, the first sound wave. The sine wave at the equator sparks life. The braiding of our DNA is like a snake, the feminine for every DNA with the masculine RNA.

Together, the 12 sound waves, counting all flats and sharps of all scales, create the template of man. The Twelve Holy Men, structures in the body, the 12 holes in the man's body, and the one extra hole for the one extra full moon, each 2.5 years representing metaphorically a woman, the womb, the room, the 13 full moon a year, of which Mary Magdalene was said to be touched by everyone, the 12 arc angles of the wheel are the 12 archangels, and this is the Star of David, the six points and six spaces. If the overlapping trinities spin, one triangle into the past, the left one into the future, a soul projecting into time and space at the center of the pyramids, fire, devotional love. Pyramid means fire within.

And the 12 decuples are the 12 disciples who create the template. Each constellation is a wavelength that creates the parts of the body. The twelve constellations, each one a vibration that creates the holographic forms of matter. If you take salt or sand on a plate and vibrate it underneath with the same hertz solfeggio lost Gregorian chant chords, you will get the sand to form a Star of David. The 12 also then create 8 possible scales times 8 notes each into our 64 codons.

Thus, we have a holographic template that starts in the womb starts with the mother and it has a placenta with the Tree of Life, Fibonacci and the fetus curls out like an amphibian then born from darkness of all knowledge of all truth of all thoughts of love, the unifying principle of all life.

Connecting all thought forms into life. Love. Peace. Mary Magdalene was the 13-diamond touched by everyone all the twelve arc angles go to the center of the wheel of life, the womb each touching the moon, the mother, the woman the room, there is the arch angels setting foot on the earth. The ankle, the foot is Neptune, spiritual offspring of God, I am as I am as Adam as an Atom with the Adams apple, meaning the word, the seeds of life, propagation is inspiration.

To stay alive in the chi form of flowing life is to be free from the concepts, to have them but they don't own you. Life is forever to be honored to be cherished, every drop of rain every ray of sun. As in born again Christians experiencing this epiphany of God. But instead, to see it as an opening to one's life force. Instead fill it with dogma.

Love is the unity of all thoughts, concepts, judgments. Love is Unity. Hate is a single thought, an ego, a limited view. The opposite of love is numbness. Hate and pain is actually love that is stuck. Unmoving, unemotional, lost. Disconnected, confused, thinking, trapped.

I got to reflect, to absorb, to take stock in this spinning into life story. This inquiry, of who am I besides a soul in a body in an eternity. Mine, a self-shining soul, self-polishing, self-cultivating adaptation mutation of this intertwining life forces, of duality. The negative and the positive. In the dark I am freed. Look at the stars they live in darkness, this truth, all surround sound, of 'hallow be thy name'. Open vessel. Self-contained. The only truth has no point. No facts or concepts can be ascertained. Spins our lives into stories as high as an empire, each one of us. Every ant, tree, and rock. Have stories. All life speaks. But it is love, the thread, the fabric of life that unites life.

I praise god's presence touches your heart, fills your soul, lets you let go of all thoughts concepts judgments and fills you with an overwhelming presence, to die for, to surrender to, to open to the home of eternity within.

God gave me this. This gift. I don't have to use it. I just am, it just is, just like a tree, wordless but mindful, voiceless but singing, speechless but productive and here the paper, the book the house, from the tree, our breath, our words, printed on a page, the forest speaks through you through me. We give a tree life. It is an exchange, symbiotic, osmosis of homeostatic existence here on earth. It's an electrical charge.

We are all together in this. Same wheel. Same planet. Humanity. Only in our hearts are we all connected to the same sound, the same song.

There is no point to life, but it is not pointless, for love is all-pervasive, yet we cannot point it out. We try to pick the apple from the garden and dissect it looking deeper and deeper just to never find the end, it goes on forever and out into space again. Love is freedom, Love is space.

The only point to life is pointless love! When we feel love, universal, personal, relational, we are experiencing all the knowledge of life into one stream, our souls getting smoother and smoother, absorbing Gods being.

The whole earth came together over one thing, Apollo 13. We all took part in something that saved this mission. Every corner of the earth, every creed, every religion was praying, was envisioning Apollo 13 back home... and it made it with a million to one odds. 1 O 1. How is one and zero the same number? The one turns, all life from the zero, a one dot a cell an atom, an Adam, the sound an Adams apple or word of god or, Word. We do not have to eat from the tree. We are the word. We are complete. Voice, sound, seeds.

Inspirit Crystals

Marcy says she is in town and looking for a house and asked me to do a tarot reading session with her. The cards I used showed a very active social life and no indications of a house for her in the near future. I let her know that I can't answer the house question, adding that I see a relationship instead. Marcy asked me to shuffle and read again.

I have had questions about which house the client should decide on, out of one or two options, and looking at address numbers, with the cards it becomes clear, but this was different, it was pointing to an entirely new love life, and she said that she has no one right now and would not know who that is. She left. So, I drew the cards, and they were filled with court cards indicating a dynamic change. I said, I don't see any houses here either. I have to say it is just about relationships. She seemed disappointed or frustrated.

I really hadn't ever come up against a zero readout. I said, "Would you like your money back because I do not see anything to do with your question at all."

Marcy said, "No, let's try again." I shuffled and she cut the deck and we did another ten-card spread. No, I still only see a significant relationship forming, but nothing about a house. Many months later in my inbox on FB page, I noticed a message but could not open at the time. Then another 6 months went by, and I finally got to those. One was Marcy. Marcy said she just wanted to let me know how she had found the love of her life and he already had a house. Marcy had moved to California with him and all her work partners at the salon were wanting me to do tarot readings for them.

Berkshire Health Retreat

At the renowned spa and retreat I worked at for ten years, I gave talks on the Fibonacci sequence of life, phi, the 5th or pentacle manifesting principle. I also did handwriting analysis at the resort. The guest would write 5 names down on a piece of paper. I could see from that who was ghosting her, who was in a conflict with her/him and why, as well as those she is closest to by movement of the alpha-bet.

In a tarot demonstration once, I set out to use the lovers card as an introduction. This card had been recently significant in that I had lost my keys at home that weekend and decided to use a card to find where I last put them. This gave me an opportunity see if pulling one single card can be prophetically as powerful by itself. It was the lovers card that surfaced. This time, the mirror that the lovers are looking into, in the background, stood out. I have seen it and used it many times indicating relationship changes and immediate interactions and the exchange of love. A mirror was in Mayril's library. I hadn't used that room recently nor that mirror, but I should go and look there. I went into the room and there they were hanging on a side hook. My mom must have put them there.

The message was clear, it pointed to the mirror. So even the cards that have a general meaning, deeper answers can come out, symbols come alive. Images connecting to the reading, to the card and back, a living vivid mental exchange, igniting the auric field visions.

They are a living book with colors and themes that let your body, which knows the answer inside anyway to access this. In our world we have lost this and it's a way to get out of the abstract by using cards and realigning with our instant knowing our instant knowledge all around us. Directly in touch with love. Love of life. Of right now flowing through us.

A couple sat down across from each other. Right away, it is only two people when most demos attract groups. The card I had decided to use in this demo, upfront, teaching how I found my keys, this way, another synchronicity. I introduced the card and talked about how it works on our auric field, absorbing and reflecting the memory fields in our bodies. At demonstrations I would use the 3-card structure, or trinity—Present, Past and Future.

The first partner shuffled; the three cards were laid down on the table. Then the other partner shuffled, but just before I gave him the deck, I shuffled them very well. I handed him the deck. He then shuffled. He then cut the deck and turned his three cards over. The cards he turned over were the exact same 3 cards that his partner had gotten, a mirror. He said that he is a mathematician and asked how many cards are in the deck. I told him 78. He said the odds of this happening are beyond configuration.

Then a person came to me while walking down the hall of the solarium. She said, "Excuse me, you won't remember me, but my sister came to you last year and she wants to relay a message to me." She continued that her sister had been transformed from ten years of grief after my session with her about the passing of her son. That I had seen and worked with her sister the year before and no one had been able to help so far. I remembered her other child, I wanted to know about that child, and it led me to the messages from her passed over child that were trying to get to her. We also did some mirror gazing. And clearing up our own thoughts on death interfering with truth. We listened in to the language of light, not the words, but sounds from the heart.

I would work summers at cottage industries for challenged special need individuals, like Sonny. Sonny had Pica. They are people that eat plastic. I was told to find something he would like to do. We were put into a small room with lots of plastic. Plastic mats, books with plastic covers, pens. I took him out of there and into the open area of the dining hall. The hall had giant round plastic tables with plastic chairs around them. I got a giant plastic pail and a sponge and filled the pail with water.

I sat down and watched Sonny washing everything perfectly clean and so happily occupied not being tempted in that other designated playroom. I presumed the aides took note and wrote it down. Weeks later, when I was called in again, I found him in the small room, where temptations abound.

For weeks I was listening to a whale call recording on a CD. Then one day, the sound finally opened my heart up so much I fell to the ground in utter appreciation of this experience. Such love, so great, so painful, my heart was feeling, stretching, expanding to this sound. Too amazing to hold it for long. I knew it would be short-lived but powerful. It taught me that anything from the heart, love or what we think is pain, is still pure love, trying to get in. Trying to open the heart, to surrender, to die to our thinking, entirely. It's as strong as an orgasm but not anything physical, all done through energy of the heart.

Two days later, I saw an article on MSN that caught my eye—usually, I do not read the news. When I opened the article, I found it was two ships crashing into each other out at sea. Sea Shepard, a Greenpeace-affiliated charity operation by Sean Penn, the famous actor, had purposefully tried to abort the mission of the Japanese boats from hunting dolphins and whales, which is strictly forbidden in the seas, but they were saying it was for research.

I noticed the time I collapsed here in New England from the whale's beautiful sound waves, thus falling to the floor filled with so much love. Like being in the womb. It read this incident occurred at 2 pm. And I calculated the proper difference in time zones and found it happened to me in synchronicity, that the ships crashed as I collapsed. A forgotten language, the language of light. The light of compassion.

I just thought maybe I had a part-time job to do. Here, on earth, to listen as a human deeply to our fellow mammals in jeopardy, out to sea and it raised the bar somehow, speculating, helps detox the world with clear visions, pure heart contemplation, and through this time music, the same sounds of these great mammals were connecting to me thousands of miles away, also intervening, an invisible life force, the mind of love churning.

Another most provocative moment was after my father's death. I was a personal assistant to a quadriplegic individual. I would at first stress before working with him of how I could influence him to feel happier. Who cares about all the work I do with him physically, what about his mental health? He had already surprised me when getting there and requesting the curtains and windows be open for him. As I did this, there was an orchestra of birds singing outside and I received a wave of happiness. I felt the feeling that I wanted him to feel. He had given it to me to cheer up. He had me cook frittata once in a while.

One day, after letting it soak and going back to scrape it with a metal spatula before using a sponge and final rinse, something seriously surprising happened. A shock.

Suddenly, out of the air, came down my father, his energy, his aura, his very soul, him, his spirit was right inside me, his very being. I said, "Dad, you are here." It was so powerful that as soon as it happened, it stopped. I thought about this juxtaposition and had to get to the bottom of it although no words are accurate and no words would ever help it happen again. I realized I believe, conjecture only, that it was the sound that called him in because after dinner each night, he would let things soak then go back into the kitchen. I could hear him scraping the pans before washing them, and this was the same sound. I thought if that is all we need to do to bring people back onto our plane then this is a cinch from here on in. Consider it done. Just remember a sound they made with something and reenact it exactly.

The bottom line, however, is that even if I had not been so shocked and he stayed here longer, this whole being, his whole soul, it did not matter. The one second was enough, I realized later, we always try to hang onto love as we do things, ideas…but they are always with us. The one second was all of him forever.

I went to the Lady of Mercy Shrine in Stockbridge and walked the stations of the cross with my six-faceted quartz crystal I had just gotten.

Suddenly, a powerful presence made me sit down, which is all very backward because it is so beautiful and surrendering and full of god's grace that no one needs to really sit down, it's just, the body reacts instantly like it is an emergency because it is so propelling into deep peace that one just needs to honor it all one can, while one can, before it leaves.

This is how I see it, being from a wild family of nine but a method was in the madness. Something is organizing all of matter and we should really appreciate her. Take time out to connect with this fact about the mystery.

I saw this over ten years, the natal chart in front of me, actually moving, the symbols, vibrating when the person came in and the chart was opened, their energy in the symbol came alive on the page as well, too.

Eventually, even astrology opens us up to beyond. It's a living ascension tool to rise to gaze the stars within, and realize they are the same ones outside of us. There is no difference. The seven days of the week, the seven chakras.

Each person is a whole universe. All the elements of the universe are in each of us. The four enzymes, YAWE, the four directions, the four elements—fire, water, air, and earth.

We can stand still and be everywhere all at once, know everything all at once, how we got here what we are and what everything is and where everything is going. IT is all accessible within, while we are in her breast in her bosom.

The mother, the dark deep receptive being we walk through and have our being.

As we walk, we cultivate more light, we grow like a star. A star on earth is a star in heaven. It's all the same place.

That's why at an investigation one does not need the evidence, or the space blocked off. When you get there and what you ask and what you see, even if it is a new thing happening, will bring in the answers needed.

If someone walks by in a shirt with a 22 on it, that will be part of the findings and these findings are the same hints given with the original evidence, no difference; if one asks, the timelines open and clues can be in the present.

Life is a living open field, we are stuck, our minds conditioned, the flow cannot reach out and through easily. Cards, prayers, meditations, chanting, and living happily unhappy merging feelings merging life force of duality all into you all into one, practicing the only singular point we have the star point the self-light our own flashlight within the womb the room the dark, the deep fertile rich black mother.

If you want to find me, you can hear me in the deep of winter, walking through the forest stepping on the small puddles of ice under my feet, crunching a crackling echo in sound, with my feet, real words of god happening.

The next person that a miracle happened with was Sarah. Sarah had had ear infections all her life and at 70 was still having to have stents put into her ears. I was doing her shoulders when suddenly, she said she felt a pop. Months later she called to tell me she had her stents out and no more ear infections.

One time, another disbeliever, came in to talk about her husband's mid-life crisis and she, I believe, did not know that in addition to astrology, I am also a medium clairvoyant psychic. In the reading, the guest mentioned how he is buying another jet and doesn't know what to upholster the seats with. For some reason, I just said out loud, "I see he has something to do with teeth."

She said, "How did you know? That is what he does for a living, dentures." She also thought I had looked her up somehow, ahead of the appointment.

I thought it would happen more, but it only happened once; the guests came in as a family and said they do not believe in what I do and wanted to try it. Right away, I felt I would not be able to do it because I had learned through one of my family members that also does not believe in it that it blocks it, and not for me, but it blocks them. They think I am not good, but what it really is, is that they are not ready for it. They have to come to it themselves to honor it in others.

They asked me specific questions and I said in my head they are talking about the father. It was something about a death and a will and they wanted me to say who it was and that they already know but they are testing me. The father came into my head, but at the same time, I was silent. Something stopped me from relaying it.

Even though I see ahead and know ahead, life still goes its way, meaning I cannot shape it. I see it.

My brother's death, I knew way ahead. When it happened, I was brought in very late at the end. The few things I tried to circumvent were blocked. Out of a large family, someone once asked if someone in our family would take their life, which one would it be? I knew exactly because of the many signs I saw leading up to it. Someone said it may be one of the other siblings who suffers from depression, but I said they speak about it so that's a no. The one that never talked about it, never said a word in that direction was the one. Humans need to talk, confront and honor their pain, honor their feelings, honor themselves. No one else will or can, forms a block.

Light is sound and sound is color. When chanting, I start to feel a sense of eternity. The chant becomes infinite. Not linear. I feel an eternal chi life force that can go on forever, and I stand in the mist of forever without moving.

The link of sound to all sound becomes space itself, her Sophia. And in the dark God said let there be light. The womb or night of all potential was first, the drawing board the back bone for The Word. The echo, the relationship, the conscious seed, of this perfect creative force was projected out. The first petals to the flower of life, from the first seed of thought, both, the positive and the negative, together, equally creating life forms. The dark gave space for form. From so-PHI-A…a form started. The PHI, the spiral of life. The Tree of Life seen in the placenta, the fingerprint, the one head, two arms two feet, 5, with the ratio of fifths. PHI. For a circle when twisted, braided like our DNA does, becomes an 8. Look at it, it is both the first petals on a flower and also the infinity of light in our eyes, the two eyes, the sun and the moon while the third inner eye, I suggest is the Holy Ghost, the medium, the glue, the thread, Mother Mary or Mary Magdelene, the true roots, the Tree of Life.

Wisdom is a woman, is Sophia. The Dark Mother of Existence. The very fabric of all life. Without Sophia, nothing would be here. Sophia created matter. The alpha and the omega. The circle of life. The embrace, the womb, room, woman, the spiral of life, the corner, all things turn, there are no straight lines. No linear thoughts are real but rabbit holes. Equal consort of truth. The two the RNA and DNA create you, me, this projected image made from all the pure potential, and from consciousness into form we can see, Gods Genesis template. The flower, the propagation.

Sight is sound the sound of wisdom, om, I am, and sound is sight, the same twisted around like the two strands of DNA, yin and yang, positive and negative, dance.

Every cell in us knows exactly where it came from, has memory, remembers how and why it is here. The thoughts get in the way of wisdom. Only deep feelings connect to this past, or Being of God, of source, to this power. The power that links us, the Holy Ghost medium, space and sound. The heart and thump, beat: of sound creating space. Awareness or consciousness creating unity, of the glue of life, love and faith.

A spark in each person is ignited, that sends the knowledge of all the cells in the body to the mind, of awareness and the whole universe fits into you. Everyone as far as it goes, this body, your body my body, every ant tree rock and rain drop has complete knowledge of or would not be here. Hear, get it, I GOD IT. U God it. WE God it. Sophia, the mother, father, God.

When I put my dad's ashes into his favorite spot, his one place on earth he loved most after traveling around the country in his blue see-through van. It was transparent from his double exposures; he had buffalo grazing in the open field then double exposed it through the next photo of his van.

There the overlapping leaves leave little room for light to come through but when it does, all the light every last separated strand of light, no matter what shape it had to come through, lands on the ground, into circles, complete round glimmering circles. Language is light. The alphabet. Alpha, Bliss. The embodiment of the soul sheds this light through writing, through our hands.

When my friend Anne died, a work partner, I went into work that day, into the house where she lived, suddenly I had to write. She came through me through writing what she wanted to say. It was many pages all of apologies but of great expression, freedom, and she was in the light communicating down to me.

Taking shorthand one hundred words per-minute certification helped. It was so much she had to say. I could keep up just barely. But I did. I was always on the edge of losing her because I could not write fast enough. But we worked together at high speeds and her message was timeless. I heard her spirit, setting free through me.

Then the dreams came. Three straight days in a row. I woke up to a dream that I said wait, this is a memory.

The flashback of the doll fumbling through Eileen's fingers and hitting the thick green tall blades of grass, and breaking into pieces, lay hidden in the lawn, lay hidden in my subconscious. The guilt I had felt one week before that my mom would kill her for not catching a doll made of fine porcelain china, had now plagued me for years and I did not put two and two together, combined, was prophetic.

Suddenly, the following weeks, I had my own life flashing back, all the things I had cut off resurfacing while in the shower. I would be four years old playing with the teal green play dough and its characteristic odor accompanying the memory, like tidal waves.

Like a reel from a film, my life returned. It came back. I reconnected with many years of absence from my emotions. Had I lost a lot, this took the fabric of my life and brought consciousness to the whole thing. Like dominoes.

Up until then, I was going on empty, but tied into spiritual feats, spiritual accomplishments, it was Eileen, she was there with me. She and I walked together. I was getting my wings to fly through her, in all my spiritual quests, because of her death. It all brought me to uncover the light within. Eileen went straight into the light, laughing all the way. The ones left here are the stories we can tell, the transformations, we experience to be reborn. To stretch our hearts, to evolve further awareness, further light.

The experience of opening to God, surrendering to the presence, needs not a single word, needs not a religion. It is religion. The hollow be thy name, the open mind, the open vessel. Be like a small child. Ask and ye shall receive, and ye shall do greater works than your Father in heaven has done, as we walk in his being and we are like him, a mirror, a reflection, the Holy Ghost; a medium, the electrical charge for light into form.

Spiders

I lived in an unfinished house, the electrical outlets had to be completed. There were a few in the kitchen, a few in the dining area and a few in the living room that the electrician said he would have to come back in a few days to finish. However, he said, he was going to leave the wires 'live' and not turn off the fuse because the fuse would shut off the other outlets that I might need. He remedied this situation by turning the wires back in on themselves into the outlet. There was a red a black and white wire at each outlet. The living room had two light switches and two plug outlets with giant loops sticking out of them. He made them safe, that way.

The next day, when I awoke and went into the living room there were four giant black spiders the size of a soft ball at each electrical outlet. I had lived in that house for many years and had seen a few wolf spiders but never anything in my whole life like this. Gargantuan is all I can say. Right away, I found myself talking directly to them, giving them a very loud and clear ultimatum. I said, "Look guys, I do not want to hurt you, but I am very uncomfortable with you here. I want you to be at the front door in the morning so I can let you out because otherwise I am not sure if I will freak out and just step on you out of fear."

I went off to Canyon Ranch to work. I came back late and went to bed. First thing in the morning, just as Temple Grandin taught me to do talk to the cows through pictures, she saw them so scared they would walk in a circle hugging the corner and figured out a way. I remember her saying use vision. So, I made sure to show the spiders me stepping frantically out of control on them if they do not go to the door by morning. Sure enough, there was one spider by the door in the morning. I got a cup and a cardboard and caught it off the wall into the receptacle and opened the door, taking it down the three steps and out across the twenty feet of lawn to the edge of the tall pine forest and let it go, throwing it out onto the pine needles.

I came back in and said, "Look, I know there are three more in here, tomorrow you better be by the door." Same thing, only one shows up and I let him out as well. The next day I said, "Alrighty, there is no spider here by the door. I am very upset." I was meditating at my bed a few hours later with a plaid blanket wrapped around my shoulders to capture the warmth over my heart chakra when suddenly, I felt a tapping, a very light almost invisible tap-tap on my shoulder.

I jumped from the bed, throwing down my blanket to the floor and looked at the corner of my bed and there he was. I had to say to myself, '*Now Brya, he did not bite you, he did not hurt you, and he just wants to say he wants out without harm.*' So, I went to grab a cup praying he'd still be in the same spot, and he was. I went to catch him and broke one of his legs by accident but continued with the mission as planned to bring him through the kitchen down the hall and out the door to the forest.

My theory is that the electrical charge from the wire and the shape that the wires were making, which resembled a spider, somehow sent messages out for mating and that these giant spiders lived far out in the forest, but could somehow sense the wires were like signals of a firefly, the sane signals given from the shape of wires into the giant spider, to propagation.

It was there too that a beetle type, a species I had never seen in my life, came into my room and I had caught it under a cup and promised it that I would be bringing it out later. I forgot and went to work. A few days later, while at work, I looked at the giant window at lunch, called the Captain's Table, and there on the window is this same species of beetle. It is like an ancient-looking flat, slow beetle. Clear as day and never any bugs on that window in the ten years I was there. "Ah ha, thank you," I told the beetle in visions in my mind, "I see what you are telling me: I forgot to let out your friend and he sent you to let me know. I hope it is not too late. As soon as I get home, I will check on him and let him go."

Three days under a cup without oxygen I thought the chances were that he had passed over, but inside I knew he was alive and with his collective consciousness he got help for himself. I turned over the cup and he moved around with his antennae, so I brought him out happily. "Go meet your friend," I said, "he's about 25 miles north, perhaps you can both travel 12.5 miles each and meet each other halfway." I have never seen that kind of beetle again.

Ending with Life

Everything is all here. Eternity is right now. Every second we are experiencing all of life, all futures, and all pasts. This is it. There is no other place to be. Right now, we are everywhere that we are ever going to be. Life is not contained in a body, a thing, a word or a name. It's a wave, that beats in the heart, the life force. Eternity is an experience of euphoria, of bliss consciousness.

It is not a distance or a concept. It is free. Open. In all directions. Pure Potential. Powerful Presence or Ambient Pure Truth, of living and being. Thus, from here to eternity is right here. You just went, and in every second, you are already there. This place, the same place, we are born, we die. This is the same exact moment of your death. Right here. Right now, is all of eternity, here and back is one instant. There is no distance, this space the entire space is all Beingness. God. Flowering Birthing Blossoming Propagating.

We are all together in this. Same wheel. Same planet. Humanity. A fabric. Thin like silk, a template. A tapestry tree in Eden, heaven is here. We hurt one thing we effect each other.

All life is alive. Every rock, tree, river forest sing. I have heard the music from the trees. The air is a living being too, a part of God, filled with consciousness. Scientists took the photons out of a tube and life still grew back in this vacuum, believe it or not, just like magic, DNA is programmed into all things, streaming.

Living the Questions

We have become subjugated to our thinking like it is all-knowing. As if a thought can come up with something beyond linear. All-knowing is the heart, the flowing of life, this is all-knowing, and love is the unity of all thought and all knowledge combined. This is love, oneness in mind, body, and soul. Love is all-inclusive. Love is whole.

We took the apple and kept analyzing deeper and deeper, learning one thing—that space is all around every atom by the millions twofold. Yet we go out into space or into the space of atoms in our hand just to come out at the same place, right here. Directing life, we think will find a final clue, but forever we look deeper and forever will be another smaller thing as long as we keep looking as long as we keep finding new powered glass amplifications times one million, we will find that atom that shows up only when we are observing, open yet to another atom again, is the same place, not a smaller particle.

It comes out the other side into space, back around in a circle. All space curves. A giant hug. Churning us to higher and higher vibrational love, frequencies. It's those corners that inertia, we think is pain, when it is a wave, it is the ride. It is the circle of life just spinning, expanding love.

I stood in the space of timelessness; never does it stop never has it begun, ageless. Up until the day we think we die; but we are always young inside. Yes, our bodies feel tired at times, but the soul inside us remains ageless. Now in the deep dark night of heaven I am awakened to the full potential of a soul in a body on a planet in a galaxy and it is a euphoria this genesis of creation.

I meditated that morning then went into the kitchen to clean. A cheerio was stuck to the floor under the table. I had to go under the table using one shoulder for holding up one corner and pry the stuck little circle of cereal off the floor with a spatula. It was stubborn. I kept saying why am I so grumpy under this table freeing up a cheerio? I should be happy. I just meditated and was just feeling joy. Where is my happiness right now when I need it? Why can't my meditation carry over to now, me under the table on one knee cleaning up cheerios?

Suddenly, as it broke into two and half propelled through the kitchen door into the living room landing by the wood stove, with one piece still stuck to the tiled floor, a wave of love went over me. That inquiry itself, the art of wondering, like a small child does, like in the Bible it says, brings us back to our innocence, was what opened my mind. The very question is a chemical mechanism to let energy flow, opening. The Cheerio, one circle stuck to the floor like glue, broken up off the floor, flew fast forward.

I didn't know I had a hummingbird for a friend. I would watch her from the giant bay window each morning scooting along the small hidden brook from bush to bush out in the distance, then meandering out of sight. One morning I had to sweep the house and missed this daily routine, engagement, my morning teatime, with her, the hummingbird, which I was assuming, only I enjoyed. Turning around by the couch, with my broom in my hands, I see her hoovering out front in the bay window as if to say where are you? Or even, instead of saying, look you spy on me, how do you like me spying in on you, table turns.

Suddenly, I could see the truth without the blinding light of our sun in my way. I could see that the very source that gave me vision also robbed me of this more all-encompassing panoramic truth. That eternity is everywhere, yet still with just the one flashlight of our sun, I was existing everywhere, in hiding. Now in the deep dark night of heaven, I am awakened to the full potential of a soul and a body on a planet in a galaxy and it is spinning.

So much of our daily life associates and links pain and fear to death. 'Look out while crossing the road; don't play with fire.' When it comes to dying, those conditioned messages are hard to separate. But death does just that. It is a wake-up call for those asleep. For life is always inviting us to experience the greater universal love in our own birth, living and death, and through others that are born, through their life and death, are we, as well, a mirror of the same thing. This is the wheel of life, the cycle, the thread through it all, that is forever evolving us.

Our hearts have many scars, all from love. It was not from an enemy. But the original link came first and foremost from our love, extending out then being hurt. This is where forgiveness can reach in and find our own love before it happened and clear away the stuck, broken love blocking us from moving on. Death does not mean to hurt us, but to wake us up. To this thread, this lifeline, beating in our chest. It can reach out, when resonating with our feelings, the heart becomes a beacon, a wave, reaching, to us and out from us, going both ways. Yet, it's all invisible. Yet, it is the only real thing alive, that is here, that we take with us, even after passing, a lifeline back to us, as it goes out to them.

Our loved ones do not mean to hurt us. This is where we are broken open, this is where all the potential lies in light getting back in. Love was always this way, here, it is an invisible threat to all existence. This is where the point of communication sits. In grief. We are perfectly imperfect like a vessel of clay, the Chinese make sure to make one small mistake on purpose, in their pottery, to let the light in. Same with our heart, when they break, even more room for expansion, for higher love, for evolution.

I learned this through a brother's death, such was to see his true soul, the light that was within him, the one I knew exactly and try and break free of my stuck-ness on how he died. As if he lingered, there was me instead—stuck—I had to set free. As soon as I saw through the pain of what I thought was painful, of his passing, I heard his joy entering me and his words were free thanking me for letting him back in, seeing his real soul, his real self, so in a pure gratitude to me, so he said he could send me where his love is now, a strong dose came to me, all through the heart. As in a birth, represents, that so called pain of the birth canal is, the mother becoming a mom, an exchange of love, seemingly linked to pain, is the essence of transformation, not pain at all but emotional power of deep connection with love. The eye-opening heart-opening awareness, to what's priority here on earth. Life, love and expanding. Standing still in peace, but powerfully moving. The arch the wave the emotion the meaning, the sentiment, the purpose, a life of love.

Heartbreaks are only from an original love. What we think is pain, is love in reverse. Love is a mirror asking one to see through the physical attachment to the higher love your partner has gone to but was also here in you, now through them, and imbibe, resonate together, this truth, this freed togetherness, that can be together at any time or place, a higher love.

Birth, life and dying are all centered around what is important, what is the essence at the core of all existence and that is LOVE, going deeper.

I had learned early on not to let conditions define me, situations to sway me, when one is focused in the heart on a universal love, stoicism, and nothing can contain us. The dying art ensues to encapsulate this courageous birth, this great moment of life we call death happens over and over to us all throughout this life through those we love who die. We must die to ourselves and learn to see them as the higher love they now are, effacing personal love into the flow of universal love, grab that hug, fill with heaven.

This is where I am perpetually sitting, residing, perched, nested in my own home, within, where my lighthouse on the sea of the soul has crashed, broken open and made new oars many times, floating and or lingering in the deep. On that precipice, on that cusp. That jumping off place from this reality into the reality of heaven on earth, within. That point of stark honesty. Of deep silence with the self. That point of embracing it all, the good and the bad, into compassionate self-love.

I, Brya, the invisible me into the visible, wanted to share with you in hopes the role of a doula is broadened to include assisting life passing over, to speaking with the other side, to caring for those processing grief, inclusive. In that fabric of universal love is the ability to commune with all of life. So just remember and respond with this new knowledge that pain in the heart or grief is because of love, that original source is still there. This hole in the heart happens so we can fill it. It's a cave, a sanctuary. We can fill it back up with our love, the love from our loved ones, the love we gave to them a sacred heightened exchange.

This is the essence of life I found here in these pages. When there is pain in the heart this is just as it sounds, a heart beating, it is another soul knocking on the door, saying, the most important thing on earth, I love you, I love you, thank you, thank you, thank you. More in a soft gentle whisper in the space between the beats. The stillness that is filled with love still tethers, their voice, their name, from here, we can hear them from anywhere in the universe, always from right now still echoing in and out of time, the beating of the heart, instills this point, this sound their voices from heaven.

Love goes right through the veil. So, memories are stored in the heart, the painful and the beautiful feelings, together. So deep a grief is triggered that it feels painful but if one has a predisposition, a discernment, a connection with how those two are really one and the same, reversed, from the other side is trying to get in, in a communication. A knocking at the door to get our attention. Then with both hands on the heart, a heart-to-heart talk reconnects true love, the love we gave to their love they still can give, speaking volumes from behind the veil. The weight of the grief is the amount of LOVE, that was shared, the potential to share again.

We need to go to the same place that we felt them before. Because all significant lasting memories are not stored in the brain but recorded in the heart. The heartbeat is the first organ to be heard at inception. The first part of the body starts developing. We never lose sight of sound, in life nor in death, it is the common thread, and as an echo in and out of our heart, again and again, does return like a kiss.

So deep a grief is triggered it's a knocking at the door, to get our attention. Sound permeates through all matter, the word of God, of om, of love. Then with both hands on the heart, a heart-to-heart talk, reconnects to our love, the love we gave, to their love the love they still can give, speaking are not a machine, but a soul, you can feel me again, our love is alive and well, from the voices in the heart.

Here. listening with the heart and all things can come through. It's heaven knocking. Its messages, still alive, wanting to come through, we can do, we can imbibe for them, for us, we have that freedom.

We tend to instead link it to a personal love, to an egoic selfish love, nothing to do with the other person, how they would feel what they would want for us. And if this is them, their only way in, through a very strong knocking, a very strong message the only way for them to get our attention. We just need to recognize that this grief is a physical learned inbuilt response in the brain, and it only takes coming down into the subtler, more emotional regions to distill and open it, again, to that real memory that real lasting feeling. This is what resides in us. But best accomplished by consciously turning love around or opening to love and letting the flow begin again, our own love ignites this.

I place both hands, not just one, but both hands on my heart, and try talking to our heart space, give love to yourself, start this way and watch the magic happen.

We all have that ability for surrender, not to be weak and more pain comes in but the key to surrendering creating a link, a thread between us and them on the other side. The light of faith gets in. Nothing can define the mystery; she has no edges, so acquiesce into the hearts ambience, the flame, light that match again.

The goal of life is to evolve our love, expand our hearts and that is what death does, now expands our awareness out, it is a stretch.

The cave of the heart, where this invisible sound, this ether, this grace can be ignited, can be uncovered, can relate to and engage, in the secret of love, it is movement, it is energy, it is touchable in our hearts, full force the one fact of life is to die to ourselves and surrender love, self-love, at this point of grief, is the healing that they want for us, to step through it, into where they went, in joy, into light, into total awareness, without limitations of the body/mind. To the purity of expansive love.

All of it is right here right in front of us, and there is nothing to get or find, we are the creative force of existence, standing still, running in circles around each day and back around. If we want to get a hold of everything, see past the framework, we can grab hold of only one thing that will get us there, love, the common thread to existence throughout the whole cosmos, this is where we travel, from the heart. The heart has energy coming in as much as going out. This apparatus expands our form, its beating waves of sound, is the first to form in the womb. The heart holds brain neuron cells and from this heart, we can communicate back and forth to loved ones gone anywhere, anyplace, anytime.

We can allow the life force of pure love to flow through us, we can allow more joy, more source, which in turn allows us to be brighter more ourselves more actively engaging in the expression of life itself. More into our life's purpose, easily. When this is opened, in the mind and in the heart, this life outside of us rushes in, we find it is also, rushing from a place inside us is also a fountain of love from inside coming out, a thread connects, we merge. We are like an empty vehicle for life to pass through. A vessel of love, the very freedom to move. Move in this mystery, this being, this great mirror before us reflecting in life and death is the same message calling us to ascend to a higher love, right here in our heart. Until then, we are unconscious, in fear. Know that we do not know, and we will find everything.

I had been meditating every day for hours on a mantra, I am one with God, and filling with a static white light. I could feel my body very weightless and even could have been levitating but there was no one to tell me. I felt like the fire in me was so ignited that I did not have to breathe. My body was circulating the power of words as vibrational sound waves, not labels, and it was the fuel to existence.

Then I found this book, '*The Secret of the Golden Flower,*' which explained exactly what I did and how it is done after I had just done it in weeks and weeks of intensive meditations at home after the sons were asleep. I even tried to get up and walk with the light into my sons' room, to bring this light within me. I felt I may not be able to disturb it or it will vanish but I did manage in a slow and graceful way to very carefully get up and walk with great mindfulness into their room—once. My ego then told me that it was not doing anything for them, as I may have thought, but doing something thought I did not know. My emotions and thoughts were at one. My body and mind were at one.

Then their voices can be heard again, their words can come through. All our heartbreaks were because of love. So, it is up to us to see the pain as a jumping-off place, an open space, a connecting link. The door is opened, the knocking stops, your grief subsides. There is a beautiful stillness, a unified peace between you both, together, communion met.

Dive into what we think and feel more deeply. It is so real on a whole new level. For now, it is an extended relationship one need not go to, but inside of us, residing in our hearts 24/7. Their love is amplified. I remember learning in art class that Chinese pottery masters would make one small mistake on purpose in the clay, as an opening for the light to get in. I have learned throughout my life, during close friend or family deaths, that in this crack, in this hole, this heartbreak, is the very same place to reach their love. That their death is also a death in us, our death in that we have to learn to die to higher love with them. For now, they are with us 24/7.

Surrendering into grief takes courage. Takes trust, takes truth, takes love, the same exact love causing the pain is the healer of the grief. Numbness is the opposite of life; numbness is the antipode.

As an arrow struck through my heart with a sharp pain at a funeral later, when I questioned, how can this be this great a pain, and said, I feel like I am dying. Behind the pain is that love in hiding, and it is up to us to bring our love to it, nurture it, hold it in a loving way and watch that it is grief which transpires, and dies, that disappears, it is pain that dies,

For love is the only thing that is real. That matters. That exalts life, its living thread.

The dying art is a creative process, at birth, during life, and at death, always inviting us to expand our minds, through our hearts, from the ego separation, of possessive love to the universal all-encompassing love, free from judgment, acceptance and honor of life itself. The mind can think, and nothing happens, unless it is a plan of action, but in the heart, it travels, while we are standing still. So, it is the deep feelings that are meaningful. Love moves life. Emotions are powerful vibrational chi force when flowing. Emotions are always birthing us from the death of our thinking, the chains of our mind. The art of birth, of life, of dying, an ever-expanding expression of love.

This is what I experienced, that the deep pain I felt, in grief, was in essence the same exact weight, of the love I had for the one passed over, reversed.

As my mother always said, put myself into other people's shoes. She came back to me when I bought those boots, two fold. The message that it is in the places of the heart that are broken that light gets in,

Our love connects to their love, unified in the heart and voices, words, feelings can be heard through our feelings again, but it flows by connecting to our hearts.

That connection still exists, love never dies, but it takes two to get there, even though they are now on the other side. It is us that blocks this flow, thinking they must be in the physical again, missing the physical attachments, we are creating fear, pain. Love is free, it is the way in, over, and through to them to the other side in the hands on our heart conveys. WE can try meeting them halfway.

Real dance on the earth lets her heart come right through our feet…so if you get the chance, open the field of love, dance on the dirt the soil the soul of Gaia as much as you can. You can feel the receptivity.

Our love takes their love, unified in the heart, and voices, words, feelings emerge like bubbles from the ocean.

The medicine of tomorrow. Sound, vibration, and tonal alignment with the earth. The inventor of Coral Castle tried leaving clues with 16 magnets and a wheel with a triangular levy. We are finding that some birds like the hummingbird and some insects like the bee and the dragonfly have heavier bodies than their wings can carry and that the sound they make is a levitational skill to keep them air-bound in order to travel.

When I experienced my brother's death, I felt even closer to him. But it took me a lot of peeling off layer after layer of my misconceptions of fear of death, blocking the real transference of love again. This can't be broken. Love is movement, love is alive. My mind blocked it. I thought it was dead. I was looking at him like he was a machine without his own light, his own peace, his own way.

This is what life is seeking in all forms, in all shapes and sizes equally—the creative life force of love is expressed openly, actively, participating like the beating of our heart.

The earth put a heart dancing in our chest and we can dance on her back and return our love, always expanding. We think it's growth, we think it is time, but it is blossoming open spaces of more and more, higher and higher love.

Epilogue

Grief, I suggest, is a calling, a voice from the heart, speaking for us to rise and go deeper, to open, to find that place, in this sacred heart space, with them again. To think we do not have to lift a finger, and to think it is a 24/7 relationship now, nothing is required to love them, only pure presence, pure compassion. This fact is hard for the linear mind to comprehend, but to put our hands together over our hearts, we can link to this living light within. It's calling us without words, to erase and be without the pain, is the key to come to the heart and feel deeper, not from the brain. A stillness where love was once exchanged, is where love remains, captured, in our hearts.

We die to ourselves, to our limited beliefs that bind us to our preconceived views, our lingering fears, purging out from the condition they died in, that tries defining them, to the allusion of death in a box, in the ground, gone, a falsity. Out from the chains of possessive love to real, pure eternal love from which we came and from whence we go, and is also deep within us, and at every heartbeat through life. Life wakes up to this cycle, rhythm, through the heartbeat. It's a call to being heartful, heart-centered, deeper feeling, sinking to a higher love, on earth, right here, while alive.

Brya at UMass BFA Graduation

Brya at Kindergarten Graduation

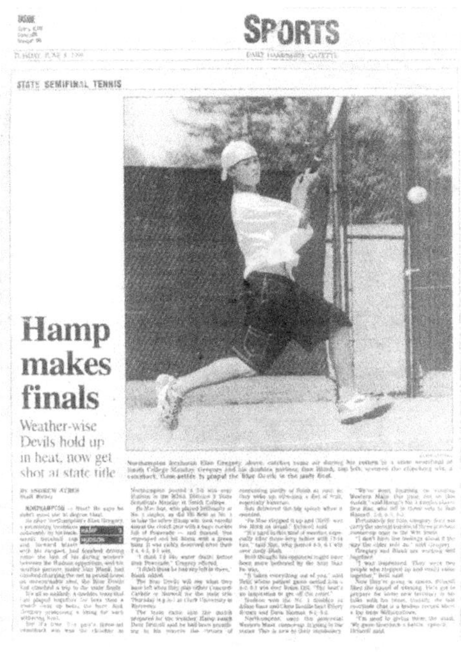

Elan at Sophia Smith Tennis Court

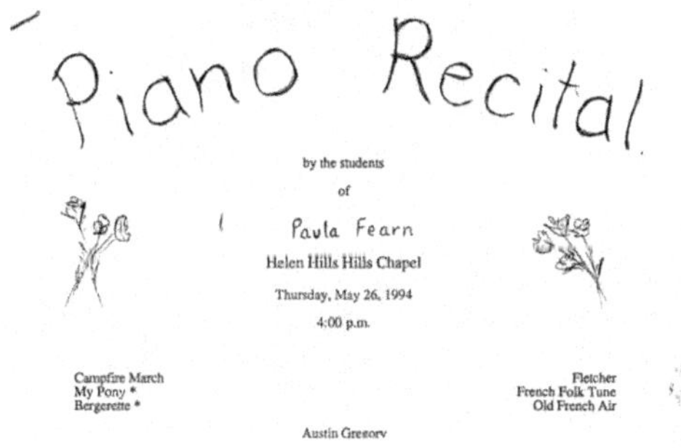

Austin at Helen Hills Piano Concert at Sophia Smith

Lady of Guadalupe Mexico Marian Apparition

Spiritual Qualities of The Tilma of Lady of Guadalupe.

1. Sash represents Virgin Pregnant with Child
2. Moon at her feet represent fertility
3. Stars on the original tilma are in the same placement as that same day December 12, 1531
4. The Tilma remains at 98.7 degrees
5. At the stomach of the Lady is a heartrate of 115 beats per minute, same rate as an infant
6. Her eyes have a vision of the Marian Apparition
7. It was in an explosion and nothing happened to it
8. There are no paint strokes
9. It never fades

Greta Thunberg

A voice from the heart came and spoke to all of us, in partnership with our planet. Greta said, "Our Houses Are On Fire." How we must stop and it's at an emergency level. S.T.A.T. Code Blue, 911.

Shortly thereafter, the earth kept going, mankind stopped in its tracks, the pandemic hit, subsequently we witnessed the skies cleared and cloudscapes that were higher and more dramatic than ever before, and I heard some endangered species were known to be revived. Gaia, our Mother Earth, was renewed, via a voice of a child. Each time a lockdown lifted, at the end of that day, I noticed small, gray-looking, smog-like clouds lining up across the horizon, looking as if the pollution coming back in was being tallied. These clogged clouds, I call them, were like an accounting, not meshed in as before, vivid and clear. There was no going back mother earth was saying. In retaliation, I am not going to digest pollution again.

Whereas, before, our pollution was being integrated and thus, hidden within our remote-controlled lives, all around us, less visible.

Thus, I named her 'Greta the Great' for one earth, one ocean, one humanity, one voice; she spoke our sacred words of wisdom on one planet, uniting us.

Recommended Resources

I Ching Book of Changes

On Death and Dying by Elizabeth Kubler Ross, M.D.

The Tibetan Book of Living and Dying by W.Y. Evan-Wentz

Open Mind Open Heart by Father Thomas Keating

Nothing Special Living Zen by Charlotte Joko Beck

Bach Flower Questionnaire

Science and Health with Key to the Scriptures by Mary Baker Eddy

Fantastic Fungi Documentary YouTube

My stroke of insight/Jill Bolte Taylor YouTube Ted Talk
https://youtu.be/UyyjU8fzEYU

10-year-old Christopher Duffley, autistic and blind singer:
https://youtu.be/-F_W_zl61bI

Earth Magic Oracle Cards by Steven D. Farmer
Goodvibes YouTube Hertz 528 Attract Miracles
Louie Giglio "How Great is Our God" YouTube

How to Talk with the Other Side:

Hands on heart, breath in 7 counts out 8 counts 3 times
Listen, feel, smell, be open, be present
Envision their face, see a memory, relive a memory

How to Talk with Trees:

Notice any animals or birds on your way there
See what direction they are flying in, north yes, south no
Feel what that is saying to you, what that brings up
Look in the sky for an eagle or a hawk when you get there
Ask the tree permission to approach closer
Stand at the tree trunk and notice its features closely
Go around the tree counterclockwise three times
Touch the tree with one hand and one hand on your heart
Ask the tree or let the tree know something or just feel
Envision another tree or place or person you want the tree
to help you with, to protect, to watch over them
In your mind, envision a few other trees the tree you
Are with can work with, even if it is miles away
If you have a group of trees, stand at the point between
Two or more trees where the equal distance is

Stand right there, where their roots comingle at the midpoint
between two trees above their roots
Stand right there and feel the electricity through your body